VAN GOGH

VAN GOGH

William Feaver

STUDIO EDITIONS

LONDON

First published in Great Britain in 1990 by Studio Editions Ltd
This revised edition published 1992 by
Studio Editions Ltd
Princess House, 50 Eastcastle Street
London W1N 7AP, England

Reprinted 1993

Additional research by Tim Ayers

ISBN 1-85170-854-5

Printed and bound in Hong Kong

Frontispiece: Self-portrait, December 1887.

INTRODUCTION

Through the tops of the trees one could see that part . . . which lies on the hill; the houses with their red roofs, uncurtained windows and green gardens; and the grey spire high above them; and below, the long grey bridge with the tall poplars on either side, over which the people passed like little black figures.

This could almost be Auvers-sur-Oise, where van Gogh stayed as Dr Gachet's patient for the last months of his life. Or somewhere near Saint-Rémy, where houses gaped by the roadside and trees were so torn between ground and sky. It is a sort of picture-book view, boldly coloured, obviously simplified, the little black figures adding animation. It was in fact Richmond-on-Thames.

Vincent van Gogh saw there what he chose to see, a setting in which he felt he could serve and thrive. It wasn't so much the actual Richmond, more the ideal place where, one bright Sunday in November 1876, he was about to preach his first sermon.

Some months earlier he had been greatly impressed by George Eliot's novel *Felix Holt*, so much so that he had sent his brother Theo a copy, urging him to read it and pass it on to their parents. Holt, a 'rough, severe fellow', dedicated his life to serving the poor. 'Preaching is your only vocation', says Esther to Felix. 'A woman doesn't like a man who tells her the truth.' She eventually marries him. Years later van Gogh was to remark that his painting *Vincent's Bedroom in Arles* (page 113) was inspired by the character of Felix Holt, by the whole tone of the book.

'Yet there were the grey steeples too, and the church-yards, with their grassy mounds and venerable head-stones, sleeping in the sunlight', Eliot wrote. 'In those midland districts the traveller passed rapidly from one phase of English life to another: after looking down on a village dingy with coal-dust, noisy with the shaking of looms, he might skirt a parish all of fields, high hedges and deep-rutted lanes.'

When van Gogh preached his first sermon he had at the back of his mind 'a delightful thought that in the future wherever I go, I shall preach the Gospel.' In essence this was true. While ceasing to be Dutch Reformed or Methodist or even Christian at all in a conventional sense, he always held to his gospel of dogged ardour. This is what makes his art uniquely direct.

Like Felix Holt he passed rapidly from one phase of life to another. Unlike other painters, he was always the amateur preacher, strong to save. His ideal artist was one who 'lived serenely as a greater artist than all other artists, designing marble and clay as well as colour, working in living flesh'. Christ was that artist; and Felix Holt the radical was Christ-like, renouncing all for 'a very bare and simple life'.

In the autumn of 1876 van Gogh was still the ex-trainee art dealer, the schoolteacher turned evangelist with no idea of becoming an artist. Richmond as he described it (in reality one of the most respectable London suburbs) was a Symbolist composition prefiguring Gauguin's Pont-Aven, a Biblical town on a hill where, he hoped, miracles would happen.

'To do this *well*, one must have the gospel in one's heart', he wrote to Theo. As one son of Pastor Theodorus van Gogh to another, he had no need to stress the importance of the sermon in a week's work, the God-given opportunity to berate, explain, inspire. 'When I was standing in the pulpit, I felt like somebody who, emerging from a dark cave below ground, returns to the light of day.'

He preached in English, naturally, and his words must have struck his Methodist congregation as strange, uncouth perhaps, but blatantly sincere.

'It is a good belief that our life is a pilgrim's progress — that we are strangers on the earth . . . our life is a long walk or journey from earth to Heaven.'

He warmed to his theme, repeating himself in order to impress upon the Richmond Methodists (and upon his brother to whom he sent the sermon, written out from memory) the full meaning, as he saw it, of his text: Psalm 119, verse 19: 'I am a stranger on earth, hide not Thy commandments from me.'

Our life is a pilgrim's progress. I once saw a very beautiful picture: it was a landscape at evening. In the distance on the right-hand side a row of hills appearing blue in the evening mist. Above those hills the splendour of the sunset, the grey clouds with their linings of silver and gold and purple . . . Through the landscape a road leads to a high mountain far, far away; on the top of that mountain is a city whereon the setting sun casts a glory.

On the road walks a pilgrim, staff in hand. He has been walking for a good long while already and he is very tired. And now he meets a woman, or figure in black, that makes one think of St Paul's words: 'As being sorrowful yet always rejoicing' . . .

Van Gogh's description, coloured by his enthusiasm, was of a painting by George Boughton, *God Speed!*,

exhibited two years before at the Royal Academy Exhibition. This was a large, prosaic study of 'Pilgrims setting out for Canterbury: time of Chaucer'. In his mind's eye van Gogh conflated the Chaucerian and the Bunyanesque. He transformed Richmond into a Jerusalem.

Twelve years later, at the start of what he called his 'campaign in the South', he said: 'The only choice I have is between being a good painter and a bad one.' His was a moral aesthetic. Good painting blazed with certainty and lingered in the memory. Bad paintings were muddled. In that 'different light' of Provence, where what he had once regarded as the 'healthy colours' of the North were replaced by 'sky blue, orange, pink, vermilion, bright yellow, bright green, bright wine-red, violet', he came to a new perception of the redeeming powers of colour. In the asylum at Saint-Rémy he made coloured versions of engravings after Doré, Delacroix, Rembrandt and Millet, adding sunshine, gold, warmth, ethereality to scenes of exhaustion, grief and dumb endurance.

Van Gogh the preacher, inspired by the graphic journalists of the London illustrated papers, 'their Monday-morning-like soberness and studied simplicity and solemnity and keen analysis', turned into van Gogh the colourist to whom nothing seemed more peaceful than yellow and blue, nothing more indicative of 'the powers of darkness' than malachite green, sulphur and red. He moved from text and illustration to a language that struck him as universal: the colours of sun, sunflowers, colours for all seasons, colours with symbolic meanings but direct impact.

He was twenty-three when he delivered his first sermon. He was to spend about five years obsessed with Bible study, evangelism, work among the poor of the Borinage in Belgium and experiencing failure. 'But I'm proof against that word failure', said George Eliot's Felix Holt. 'The only failure a man ought to fear is failure in cleaving to the purpose he sees to be best.' Turning to drawing, gradually clarifying his ideas about art, he reassured himself that the act of delineation is in its way redemptive. All things become simply crayon or ink on paper. 'If one draws a willow as if it were a living being – and after all, it really is – then the surroundings follow in due course if one has concentrated all one's attention only on that same tree, not giving up until one has put some life into it.'

Van Gogh's career as preacher-turned-artist lasted ten years. For more than half that time he trained himself and translated his ideas, uncertain as to where they would lead him. By 1883 he felt he knew his way. 'I have found in my work something which I can devote myself to heart and soul, and which inspires me and gives a meaning to life,' he wrote to Theo. 'I have a firm *faith* in art, a firm confidence in its being a powerful stream which carries a man to a harbour.'

The Carpenter's Yard and Laundry, 1882.
Pencil, brush, heightened with white, 28.5 × 47 cm
Rijksmuseum Kröller-Müller, Otterlo

The pilgrim progressed. The appeal of his faith in art lay in its demands: constant practice, perpetual endeavour to be truthful. But he took with him, from Sunday school teaching into art, certain assumptions. He took the most blatant images of death-in-life, of growth, fulfilment, of harvest and renewal, and presented them whole. Each field, each tree, each person confronted for portrait purposes signified an attempt to grasp essentials. The presence of the pair of boots, the sunflowers, the nests and baskets, the stalwart chair, the village cowering with rain striking down, was both illustrative and illuminating.

'It was a clear autumn day and a beautiful walk from here to Richmond along the Thames' he wrote to Theo, describing how the day he preached his 'God Speed!' sermon had gone. That afternoon, while still only an occasional sketcher, the life of van Gogh the artist began.

Through van Gogh's eyes, through his impassioned speed (particularly in his last months), through his lavish use of 'sky blue, orange, pink, vermilion, bright yellow, bright green, bright wine-red, violet', through

The Yellow House in Arles, 1888.
Chalk, pen, brown ink, watercolour, 25.5 × 31.5 cm
Vincent van Gogh Foundation,
Vincent van Gogh Museum, Amsterdam

his letters and through his expository zeal, an unprecedented sort of painting came about. To reach into the hearts of his congregation young van Gogh resorted to ringing quotations and straightforward, confessional appeals. In his paintings he eventually did the same, moving from scenes of labour and hardship, such as he had seen from time to time in *The Graphic*, to images that had moral presence. The subject matter was not, in itself, remarkable. At the 1874 Royal Academy, in Goupil's, in The Hague, he found plenty to impress him. At the Paris Salon, in the Luxembourg gallery too, he saw paintings of the humble peasant, the daily task, shepherding, husbandry, the small pleasures of simple lives and the long dullness of grief. His versions of such art were often shocking because they were so unrefined, so lacking in finesse. In other words, van Gogh went beyond Millet – who never neglected to show that he was, after all, highly skilled, however lowly his motifs – by becoming so direct a painter.

Starry Night (page 107), painted in June 1889: 'The olives with white cloud and background of mountains, as well as the rising moon and *the impression of night*, are exaggerations from the point of view of arrangement, the lines being distorted like those in old woodcuts.' Starting with the plain statements and glaring verdicts of English picture-journalism as his guide, van Gogh developed an instinct for the ground swell and the rising sap. The weightiness of his stooping miners, the women bent under sacks of coal, the vigour of the wheat stooks, the rhythmic thump of women taking to the floor in the Antwerp dance hall, show him quickening in response. The paintings of nests and baskets, potatoes, a skull and Père Tanguy seated like a down-to-earth Buddha against a backdrop of sketchy Japanese prints, reveal his self-taught ability to do without the correctitude of the fully-trained. Suddenly, and unhesitatingly, he puts life into them.

Van Gogh retained his humility. He remained convinced, to the end, that he was a lesser artist than Gauguin, not least because Gauguin told him so. It was the humility of the former preacher (rather than, in Gauguin's case, the former stockbroker) and it meant that copying was more than a useful exercise. It was a form of recitation or restatement. The aim in

art was to achieve the repeatability of a well-known, well-loved poem. In his sermon to the Richmond Methodists he recited part of Christina Rossetti's poem *Up-hill*:

Does the road wind up-hill all the way?
Yes, to the very end.
Will the day's journey take the whole long day?
From morn to night, my friend.

The graphic artists he admired – artists like Hubert Herkomer and Luke Fildes – were famous for the immediacy of their illustration and reportage. Fildes drew Charles Dickens' study at Gad's Hill the morning after his death: the place where *The Mystery of Edwin Drood* was never to be resolved, where the author's chair was left empty. Van Gogh had that image in his thoughts when he painted his own rough, severe chair, and Gauguin's more elaborate one, in the Yellow House in Arles.

Fildes went on to become one of the most popular late nineteenth-century painters in England and America, largely on the strength of one painting, of which a photogravure, published in 1892, sold phenomenal numbers of copies. *The Doctor*, commissioned in 1887 and exhibited at the Royal Academy in 1891, was – unknown to van Gogh – the last and greatest of what might be termed the Felix Holt genre. The doctor attends the sickbed, possibly the deathbed, of a child. The bed is improvised, on two chairs. The doctor sits, waiting. The emblems of sickness – medicine bottle, jug, lamp still burning as dawn comes, bird in cage, and the child's own small chair already empty, are all around. This picture, composed with immense care, painted in a specially built mock-up cottage, was worked on, start to finish, during the years in which van Gogh moved from Paris to Arles, to Saint-Rémy and, finally, to Auvers.

The difference between one, high-resolution, studio-based bid for universal sympathy and all those other paintings van Gogh produced in that time, is more

Red Vineyards at Arles, *1888.*
Oil on canvas, 75 × 93 cm
Pushkin Museum, Moscow

The Dance Hall at Arles, *1888.*
Oil on canvas, 65 × 81 cm
Musée d'Orsay, Paris

Women Carrying Coal, 1882.
Watercolour, 32 × 50 cm
Rijksmuseum Kröller-Müller, Otterlo

than strikingly coincidental. It marks the distance that grew between van Gogh's literary inspired ideas and his directly inspired painting. *The Potato Eaters* of 1885, based on studies of the De Groot family, is the closest he got to the set-piece methods of *The Doctor*. Van Gogh was absorbed most of the winter months of 1885 undertaking preliminary sketches of the scene, drawing gnarled outstretched hands and intense bright-eyed faces.

Moving away from the north, first to Paris and then to the Midi, meant that he lost contact with that sort of tableau painting. Those he met in Paris, notably Pissarro, stimulated him to impatience with such exhaustively plotted motifs. He learnt to rely not on a dramatist's chiaroscuro but on the vibrancy and power of colour.

Women Carrying Coal, *1882.*
Watercolour, 32 × 50 cm
Rijksmuseum Kröller-Müller, Otterlo

'By intensifying *all* the colours one arrives once again at quietude and harmony.'

At the end of Zola's *L'Œuvre*, a novel van Gogh read soon after it was published in 1886, the painter Claude Lantier (a character part Édourd Manet, part Paul Cézanne, as Zola saw them) commits suicide and is buried in Avenue 3 of a 'vast flat cemetery, still quite new', where the priest's '*Revertitur in terram suam unde erat*' is drowned out by the snorts of a shunting engine, on the embankment overlooking the cemetery.

It had rained so heavily during the past few days, and the earth was so very soft, that one side of the grave suddenly fell in and one of the grave-diggers had to jump down and clear it with his spade; which he did with slow rhythmic gestures that seemed likely to go on for ever, greatly to the annoyance of the priest . . . Up on the embankment the railway engine was in action again, backing and blasting out showers of red-hot cinders into the dull grey sky.

Van Gogh's paintings often serve as descriptions. There are railways bringing modernity to the timeless rural scene. There are odd juxtapositions: the harvest fields rolling towards the horizontal billows of steam from the passing train. In the literary work of Zola and Maupassant, van Gogh found the telling contrasts he loved, the constant signs of wider or darker possibilities lurking behind the seemingly ordinary appearances of everyday life.

Zola's *Germinal*, the mining community drama set – in effect – in van Gogh's Borinage, is in black and grey relieved only by the warmth of family and friendships, and by the torch of goodness, the small beacons of self-sacrifice. The factual side of Zola related him to the *Graphic* artists. His other aspect, his virtuosity, was more Manet, more Frans Hals.

As far as van Gogh was concerned, Frans Hals was admirable not just because his technique was so vivid ('hands that lived, but were not finished in the sense they demand nowadays') but for his concentration on his subject.

He never painted Christs, annunciations to the shepherds, angels, crucifixions or resurrections; he never painted nude, voluptuous and bestial women . . .
He did portraits, and nothing, nothing else.

Writing to Emile Bernard (the painter he felt closer to in terms of Symbolism), van Gogh insisted that Hals alone of the Dutch masters knew not only how to paint ('no less than twenty-seven blacks') but what was right to paint.

'It is as beautiful as Zola, healthier as well as merrier, but as true to life, because his epoch was healthier and less dismal.'

When van Gogh left Paris for Arles he went in the hope of finding a healthier calmer life, away from the overbearing pressures that were gradually turning him into an alcoholic, away from the numerous distracting artists with their competitive instincts and in his opinion, inflated egos. He left Paris in order to find suitable locations and worthwhile sitters to paint.

Virtually the first person he met in Arles was Joseph Roulin, the station postal official. He sat for van Gogh, for something to do. ('He lives a great deal in

Portrait of the Artist's Mother, 1888.
Oil on canvas, 39 × 30.5 cm
Norton Simon Art Foundation, Los Angeles

Mademoiselle Gachet in her Garden, 1890.
Oil on canvas, 46 × 55 cm
Musée d'Orsay, Paris

cafés and is certainly more or less a drinker . . . but he is so much the reverse of a sot, his exaltation is so natural, so intelligent and he argues with such sweep.') Roulin was a Hals figure, and van Gogh painted him as such. Where Hals had satin and ruffs to deal with, van Gogh had the rough serge and the peaked cap. He set Roulin in a chair, the inveterate republican prepared to argue. He put him against wallpaper, his beard as luxuriant as the patterning. He painted the whole Roulin family, parents and children, one by one.

'What appeals to me most . . . is the portrait, the modern portrait.'

Joseph Roulin, Armand Roulin, Camille Roulin, Madame Augustine Roulin (*La Berceuse*) and baby

Marcelle Roulin were all that he had hoped for. He idealized them, describing to Emile Bernard the affection Joseph felt for the baby, his tenderness and consideration. Roulin helped him after the crisis of December 1888 when he had his breakdown. The Roulins were a nestful of characters. When he couldn't paint them, or others such as Lieutenant Milliet, the Zouave, or the doctor at Arles hospital or his doctor and warder at Saint-Rémy, Dr Gachet and Dr Gachet's daughter, he had to paint himself. When that palled, and weather allowed, he went out to paint the countryside instead. Or there were the various forms of still-life: the table-top arrangement, the flowers, the vegetables available.

'I think a great lesson taught by the old Dutch masters is the following: to consider drawing and colour one.'

In Antwerp he had observed how Rubens drew the lines in his faces 'with streaks of pure red'. The energy of Hals, he noted, lay in the darting, tweaking brushstrokes. Painting lemons or potatoes, he drew outlines and shadowing in lemon yellow and dirty ochres. He learnt to exaggerate, to see places as spiritually golden or scarlet or sulphurous, and to colour them as such.

In Paris, seeing how Pissarro dabbed and Seurat flecked, he had been conscious of being the Northerner learning to paint lightly. In Arles he was the lone explorer, not so much the missionary as the venturesome topographer annexing the territory – and a few of the locals – for his purposes. The 'campaign in the South' was an overnight journey in the general direction of the exotic. It wasn't Japan, but it was more Japanese than Nuenen.

Arriving to find snow, he reminded himself of views of Mount Fuji and Japanese back yards with the cane fences and cherry trees framing every vista. Japan, known to him through prints and hearsay, represented harmony. There, he believed, peasants and artists fitted effortlessly together into the scheme of

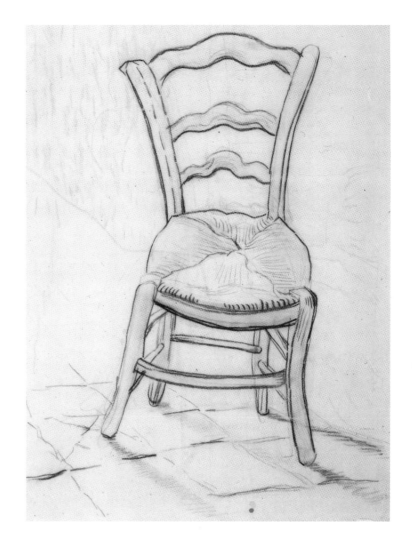

The Chair, *1890.*
Pencil drawing, 33 × 24.5 cm
Vincent van Gogh Foundation,
Vincent van Gogh Museum, Amsterdam

things. The land was the perfect backdrop. Art was everyday. The prints that served as wrapping paper were images of a society in which the artist's calling was similar to that of a monk. If the Dutch masters had taught him to treat colour and line as one, the Japanese implied, for him, an even more complete aesthetic: one of dramatic cohesion. Abrupt close-ups and landscapes snowy blank or sliced with rain superimposed themselves on the faces he studied and the fields he walked through. Out on the road to Tarascon, passing among the smallholders of the Crau, he translated as he went. Spring turned into

Garden in Provence, *1888.*
Pen drawing, 49 × 61 cm
Collection Oskar Reinhart, Winterthur

Meadow with Butterflies, *1890.*
Oil on canvas, 64.5 × 91 cm
National Gallery, London

summer, the corn grew; the maddening mistral sharpened the light, scouring as it blew, making a day's work outdoors difficult if not impossible.

As van Gogh learnt the vocabulary of the Crau, drawing it with a reed pen, devising a shorthand for fence and irises, rocks and stubble, he became confident as never before. Here at last was a stretch of land that (although it reminded him of de Koninck, the Dutch master of horizontality) he could declare his. Through the summer of 1888 he annexed what suited him, from Montmajor to Les Saintes-Maries-de-la-Mer, painting as fast as he could in order to seize hold. 'Quick souls', George Eliot says in *Felix Holt*, 'have their intensest life in the first anticipatory sketch of what may or will be.'

'*Admire* as much as you can; *most people do not admire enough*' was van Gogh's advice to his brother in 1874. Admiration lay behind the curious opposites in his style. There were the Japanese prints, admired because they seemed to represent a perfect, stylistic solution to social problems. There were the crusty, turgid paintings of Monticelli: 'What a mistake the Parisians make in not having a palette for crude things, for Monticellis, for common earthware.' Gauguin (admired for his forcefulness by van Gogh) despised thick paint, and the idea that 'common earthenware', or its painterly equivalent, should be appreciated on clumsy moral grounds. But then most of van Gogh's ideas ('I can't help liking Meissoniers') were based on early loyalties and obstinate likings. They were shaped in isolation.

Van Gogh's Symbolism (the enlarged sun, the nest woven into the branch, the billowing wheat-field enclosed by a wall) was inspired more by the metaphors of the Psalms than by other art. Yet, as an almost entirely self-taught painter, and as a draughtsman who had failed every test, by Antwerp Academy criteria, he longed for a common language in which he could (trilingual as he already was) communicate fluently.

More and more it seems to me that the pictures which must be made so that painting should be wholly itself, and should raise itself to a height equivalent to the serene summits which the Greek sculptors, the German musicians, the writers of French novels reached, are beyond the power of an isolated individual; so they will probably be created by groups of men combining to execute an idea held in common.

Style would reconcile. Style would be attuned to overwhelming impulse. Wagnerian, so to speak. ('What an artist . . . one like that in painting would be something. *It will come*.') Gauguin and he would begin an artists' settlement in Arles. The Yellow House would become an outpost of the new serenity, a solar cell, a spiritual abode.

'Painting ought to be done at the public expense, instead of the artists being overburdened with it', he wrote to Theo in August 1888. Van Gogh's painting, of course, was done at his brother's expense. Money for subsistence, tubes of paint in sufficient quantity for him to paint quicker than Monticelli but just as thickly, were the essential accompaniment to Theo's replies to Vincent's letters. The relationship of the brothers was, theoretically, that of artist and dealer.

The van Goghs were eminent over two generations in the Netherlands, as important figures in the art trade. Vincent's failure as a dealer and his re-emergence, after the wilderness years of evangelism, as the family artist (in succession to Anton Mauve, related to his mother by marriage) could be rationalized as a false start followed by long-term investment in his talent. But Theo's support was, as they both knew, far more than that. Theo arranged Gauguin's move to Arles; Theo listened; Theo allowed himself to become the recipient of Vincent's outpourings. 'My work is my body and soul, and for it, I am risking my life and my reason.'

The letters van Gogh wrote, to his mother and sister, to Bernard and Gauguin and most of all – more than

Pollard Willows and Setting Sun, *1888.*
Oil on canvas, 31.5 × 34.5 cm
Rijksmuseum Kröller-Müller, Otterlo

650 of them – to Theo, turn the paintings into illustrations. Without their running commentary the dates would be uncertain and the intentions would be, more often than not, unstated. The letters exist because van Gogh moved from home, from the Netherlands and, eventually from Paris. They throw his beginnings as an artist, and his final years, into unique focus. Where Delacroix's journals are relatively chatty, van Gogh's letters address themselves to constant emergencies. They also have something of the confessional tirelessness of the journals that ended on June 22nd 1846:

God forgive me. Amen
Finis
of
B.R. Haydon
'Stretch me no longer on this rough world' Lear
End of Twenty-sixth Volume.

Haydon, after a lifetime of, as he saw it, unjust neglect by ruling Academicians and art patrons, slit his throat, leaving his journals as a monument to unrequited ambition. Van Gogh's letters are in some ways equivalent to Haydon's eloquent outpourings. They confess his aspirations and list his setbacks. Yet unlike Haydon, van Gogh had no vanity or self-pity. His letters demanded – and received – response. The solicitude (and francs, paint and canvas) that came by return was vital to him. For although he felt increasingly guilty about imposing on Theo, he could regard his brother as his keeper, his receiver. Theo, in a sense, stood in for posterity and, as he predicted, posterity owes much to Vincent. He said: 'I should not be surprised if my brother were one of the great geniuses and will one day be compared to someone like Beethoven.'

The long conversations-turned-monologues that Vincent held with Theo, writing to him at night, involved descriptions of work accomplished and about to be despatched to Paris, and accounts of what he longed for or planned to do. The letters were substitutes for proper conversations, such as had exhausted Theo when Vincent lived with him in Paris. They reflect his energy, particularly on those days when work went well, days, he reported, when 'the brushstrokes come like clockwork'.

Sometimes such elation was ominous, for van Gogh worked towards the deadlines of nervous crises. There was panic at the thought of intrusion or change, and depression at Christmas. But he also speeded up when the mood seized him, when the irises nodded at him, the fields shivered and the sun brought on the harvest.

A size 30 canvas (roughly 70 by 90 cm) could be carried easily enough along the road to a chosen spot, and a painting could result in a matter of hours. Tube paints made such rapidity possible. Straight from the tube, often unmixed, his cobalt skies and carmine poppies, raw yellows and greens were the fruits of alacrity. Even when he sat and considered (as in *The Night Café* or *Vincent's Bedroom*) the intention remained: to achieve in his rough and ready way what Frans Hals had made to seem spontaneous.

There was a lack of snobbery in van Gogh's talkative approach. His openness, a goodness verging on naivety that Gauguin especially found intolerable, was the lasting basis of his whole style. No one else would have admitted – in Post-Impressionist circles – to admiring both Meissonier and Monticelli. He painted as he wrote and as he had preached, always in direct speech. He addressed himself to particular subjects ('The cypresses are always occupying my thoughts'), trying them out in words and sketches. 'Cypresses which show off their nightmarish silhouettes of black flame; mountains which rear their backs like mammoths or rhinoceroses.' In his exaltation he echoed the psalmist's 'mountains skipped like rams and the little hills like lambs'.

'Vincent and I simply cannot live together in peace

St Paul's Hospital, Saint-Rémy, *1889.*
Oil on canvas, 63 × 48 cm
Musée d'Orsay, Paris

because of incompatibility', Gauguin wrote to Theo at the end of the attempt to achieve creative harmony in the Yellow House in Arles. Van Gogh's breakdown, during Christmas 1888, was brought on by Gauguin, by anxiety, perhaps, at Theo's marriage and divided responsibilities, by his remedies ('the only way . . . is to stun myself with a lot of drinking or heavy smoking') and the underlying urgency of painting after painting.

'I am caught in the wheels of the Fine Arts, like wheat between the millstones', he had written to Theo in the summer of 1888. From then onwards he was ground down by the fear of madness. The period in the Arles hospital followed by a whole year at Saint-Rémy (May 1889–May 1890), relieved him of the day-to-day difficulties of providing for himself but the strain of being an inmate aggravated his disorder. He argued to himself that circumstances could be worse. 'By seeing the actual *truth* of the life of these various lunatics and crazy folk I am losing the vague dread, the fear of the thing.'

Painting the view from his upstairs cell, the field seething to the boil, the mountain enlarged and closing in, van Gogh saw the seasons accelerate, growth one day, stubble the next. 'Life's so short, and especially the number of years in which one's strong enough to risk everything'.

The weeks in which he could not work were death to him: blank weeks when Dr Peyron noted 'acute mania with generalized delirium'. Those weeks broke the continuity of nearly ten years. Yet, 'the peasant *must* be a peasant, that digger *must* dig': he revived himself with exercises, making copies from reproductions after Delacroix, Millet and Doré. He added colour and a good-natured burliness to Millet's scenes from peasant life. He began to consider returning to the homelands of the north.

In his lucid periods ('the unbearable hallucinations have ceased, and are now getting reduced to simple nightmares') he was allowed out, under supervision. He found in the Alpilles a primordial landscape, a path leading into 'Les Peyroulets', a honey-combed, worm-eaten ravine. The convulsive rocks, worn away by the stream, blended with the grey skies of his Netherlands, thatched houses in lumpy villages, places distanced and generalized as he remembered or imagined them.

To go to live in Auvers-sur-Oise for a while was a sensible plan, for there the sympathetic Dr Gachet could keep an expert eye on him, Theo and his wife were within reach, and in the placid North no mistrals blew.

Street in Auvers-sur-Oise, *1890.*
Oil on canvas, 73 × 92 cm
Ateneum, Antell Collection, Helsinki

Thatched Cottages in Auvers, *1890.*
Oil on canvas, 65 × 81 cm
Kunsthaus, Zürich

Van Gogh's Auvers period lasted only long enough for him to paint the one season, springtime to high summer, from blossom to reaping. 'The greatest, most powerful imaginations have at the same time made things directly from nature that strike one dumb': in Auvers he studied Daubigny's garden, and painted it, in homage to the painter who had, like Constable, shown that there was nothing too lowly in nature to be worth painting. He painted where Cézanne and Pissarro had been.

Awareness of this did not inhibit him and Auvers soon danced to his rhythm. He moved from church to street to chestnut trees in bloom. He painted Dr Gachet's portrait (describing it to Gauguin as having 'the heartbroken expression of our time') and he moved out into the fields, unaccompanied.

The landscape of the Oise valley was all green and shallow, he found. But there it was and for some weeks (the painter *must* paint) he made the best of it.

Harvest-time again and, for 'the sower of God's word', momentary fulfilment. Two years earlier he had written to Emile Bernard: 'I am still charmed by the magic of hosts of memories of the past, of a longing for the infinite, of which the sower and the sheaf are the symbols.'

Now, even now, he could remember perhaps the circumstances of his first sermon. 'It was a clear autumn day and a beautiful walk from here to Richmond along the Thames, in which the great chestnut trees with their load of yellow leaves and the clear blue sky were mirrored,' he had written to Theo in 1876 as he began.

'On the road walks a pilgrim, staff in hand. He has been walking for a good long while already and he is very tired. And now he meets a woman, or figure in black, that makes one think of St Paul's words: "*As being sorrowful yet always rejoicing*".'

'Well, the truth is, we can only make our pictures speak'
(Letter to Theo, July 1890)

LETTERS

The following extracts are taken from *The Complete Letters of Vincent van Gogh, with reproductions of all the drawings in the correspondence*, 3 vols, NYGS and Thames and Hudson, 1958.

Letter 473, Arles, 1888

Shortly after his arrival in Arles in February 1888, van Gogh wrote to his brother to arrange for the distribution of various works among Dutch friends and dealers, throwing light on his perception of himself at this period, after his stay in Paris, as an Impressionist:

One thing remains not so easily settled, since Tersteeg [a Dutch dealer] has written to you, 'Send me some Impressionists, but only those pictures that you yourself think the best', and since you for your part sent a picture of mine in that batch, I find myself in the not very easy position of having to convince Tersteeg that I am actually a genuine Impressionist of the Petit Boulevard, and that I intend to remain so.

Well, he shall have a picture of mine in his own collection. I have been turning it over in my mind these days and I have thought of an odd thing, not like what I generally do. It is the drawbridge with the little yellow cart and the group of women washing linen, a study in which the ground is bright orange, the grass bright green and the sky and water blue.

Drawbridge with Carriage

Painted 1888
54.5 × 65 cm
Rijksmuseum Kröller-Müller, Otterlo

Letter 478, Arles, 20 April 1888

The correspondence between Vincent and Theo reveals the artist's total financial dependence upon his brother. In this letter, van Gogh is busy with a series of canvases on the theme of orchards in bloom. Many of the letters, including the present example, are decorated with sketches of compositions on which he was working:

Thank you for your letter of today, and for the 100-franc note it contained. As for the earlier letter with the 50 francs, I got it too, and I wrote to you about it the day, or two days, before I sent the two drawings . . .

I have ten orchards now, not counting three little studies, and one big one of a cherry tree which I have spoiled . . .

These orchards, with the Pont de l'anglais [sic], will make a first series. If you would rather leave them to dry out here, perhaps it would be as well. They are now on a covered terrace to dry . . .

Here is a sketch of an orchard that I planned for you to celebrate 1 May [Theo's birthday]. It's absolutely clear, and done all at once. A frenzy of impastos of the faintest yellow and lilac on the original white mass.

You will probably be in Holland by then, and perhaps you will be seeing the same trees in flower there on that very day . . . .

Orchard with Blossoming Plum Trees

Drawn 1888
39.5 × 54 cm
Vincent van Gogh Foundation,
Vincent van Gogh Museum, Amsterdam

Si tu préfèrès que cela sèche encore ici cela n'est pas mauvais peutêtre. Ils sont maintenant sur une terrasse couverte pour y sécher

Dites donc Daumier est exposé aux Beaux arts & Gavarni n'est ce pas Bravo pour le Daumier pas pour les Beaux arts

Bleu

arbre vert

tout orange

carré vert

terrain

lilas

+ Mon cher Theo, Merci de ta lettre d'aujourd'hui et du billet de 100 fr. qu'elle contenait. Pour ce qui est de la précédente contenant 50 fr je l'ai également reçue et je te l'ai aussi écrit le jour avant ou deux jours avant que je n'aie envoyé les deux dessins. Ces dessins sont faits avec un roseau taillé comme serait une plume d'oie. je compte en faire une série comme cela. et j'espère faire mieux que les deux premiers. C'est un procédé que j'ai déjà cherché en Hollande dans le temps, mais là je n'avais pas d'aussi bons roseaux qu'ici. Ai reçu une lettre de Koning de laquelle veuille le remercier. très volontiers je veux lui échanger les deux dessins contre une étude de lui que tu choisiras & garderas dans ta collection. Je lui écrirai pour lui expliquer le procédé et lui enverrai des roseaux taillés pour qu'il puisse en faire aussi. Maintenant c'était une importante nouvelle que celle de ton voyage à Bruxelles.

Letter 520, Arles, summer 1888

In Arles, Vincent took a keen interest in portraiture, and his perception of himself as an artist underwent a change. He wrote to Theo:

You are shortly to make the acquaintance of Master Patience Escalier, a sort of 'man with a hoe', formerly cowherd of the Camargue, now gardener at a house in the Crau. The colouring of this peasant portrait is not so black as in the 'Potato Eaters' of Nuenen [p.47], but our highly civilized Parisian Portier . . . will be bothered by the same old problem. You have changed since then, but you will see that he has not, and it really is a pity that there are not more pictures en sabots *in Paris. I do not think that my peasant would do any harm to the de Lautrec in your possession if they were hung side by side, and I am even bold enough to hope the de Lautrec would appear even more distinguished by the mutual contrast, and that on the other hand my picture would gain by the odd juxtaposition, because that sun-steeped, sunburned quality, tanned and air-swept, would show up still more effectively beside all that face powder and elegance.*

What a mistake Parisians make in not having a palate for crude things, for Monticellis, for common earthenware. But there, one must not lose heart because Utopia is not coming true. It is only that what I learned in Paris is leaving me, and I am returning to the ideas I had in the country before I knew the Impressionists. And I should not be surprised if the Impressionists soon find fault with my way of working, for it has been fertilized by Delacroix's ideas rather than by theirs. Because instead of trying to reproduce exactly what I have before my eyes, I use colour more arbitrarily, in order to express myself forcibly. Well, let that be, as far as theory goes, but I'm going to give you an example of what I mean.

I should like to paint the portrait of an artist friend, a man who dreams great dreams, who works as the nightingale sings, because it is his nature. He'll be a blond man. I want to put my appreciation, the love I have for him, into the picture. So, I paint him as he is, as faithfully as I can, to begin with.

The Old Peasant, Patience Escalier
Painted 1888
64 × 54 cm
Private Collection

But the picture is not yet finished. To finish it I am now going to be the arbitrary colourist. I exaggerate the fairness of the hair, I even get to orange tones, chromes and pale citron-yellow.

Behind the head, instead of painting the ordinary wall of the mean room, I paint infinity, a plain background of the richest, intensest blue that I can contrive, and by this simple combination of the bright head against the rich blue background, I get a mysterious effect, like a star in the depths of an azure sky.

Again, in the portrait of the peasant I worked this way, but in this case without wishing to produce the mysterious brightness of a pale star in the infinite. Instead, I imagine the man I have to paint, terrible in the furnace of the height of harvest-time, as surrounded by the whole Midi. Hence the orange colours flashing like lightning, vivid as red-hot iron, and the luminous tones of old gold in the shadows

Oh my dear boy . . . and the nice people will only see the exaggeration as a caricature . . .

Letter 537, Arles, 17 September 1988

My dear Theo,
Probably I shall hear from you tomorrow morning, but I
have time to write to you tonight, and the week has been
rather eventful.

I am convinced that in the end we shall do well by
furnishing the studio. Already I feel freer in my work, and
less harried by unnecessary annoyances than I have been.

Only if, as I hope, I take more pains with the style and
quality of my work, it will go a little more slowly, or rather
I shall have to keep the pictures with me longer. That is, if
they are subjects that are connected and complement each
other. And also because there will be some pictures which I
certainly do not want to send you till they are bone dry.

In this last category there is a square size 30 canvas, a
corner of a garden with a weeping tree, grass, round
clipped cedar shrubs and an oleander bush. The same
corner of the garden, that is, which you already had a
study of in the last parcel. But as this one is bigger, there is
a citron sky over everything, and also the colours have the
richness and intensity of autumn. And besides it is in even
heavier paint than the other one, plain and thick. That is
picture number one this week.

The second represents the outside of a café, with the
terrace lit up by a big gas lamp in the blue night, and a
corner of a starry blue sky [page 81].

The third picture this week is a portrait of myself,
almost colourless, in grey tones against a background of
pale malachite.

I purposely bought a mirror good enough to enable me
to work from my image in default of a model, because if I
can manage to paint the colouring of my own head, which
is not to be done without some difficulty, I shall likewise
be able to paint the heads of other good souls, men and
women.

The problem of painting night scenes and effects on the
spot and actually by night interests me enormously. This
week I have done absolutely nothing but paint and sleep
and have my meals. That means sittings of twelve hours,
six hours and so on, then a sleep of twelve hours at a
stretch . . .

Public Garden with Round Clipped Shrub and Weeping Tree (The Garden of the Poets)

Painted 1888
73 × 92 cm
The Art Institute of Chicago

Letter 543, Arles, September 1888

Still waiting for Gauguin, van Gogh describes to Theo *Starry Night* (page 107) and a sketch for the painting of his own house in Arles. Only the wind, the mistral, disturbs his application.

. . .

Enclosed a little sketch of a square size 30 canvas, the starry sky actually painted at night under a gas jet. The sky is greenish-blue, the water royal blue, the ground mauve. The town is blue and violet, the gas is yellow and the reflections are russet-gold down to greenish-bronze. On the blue-green expanse of the sky the Great Bear sparkles green and pink, its discreet pallor contrasts with the harsh gold of the gas.

Two colourful little figures of lovers in the foreground.

Also a sketch of a size 30 canvas representing the house and its surroundings in sulphur-coloured sunshine, under a sky of pure cobalt. The subject is frightfully difficult; but that is just why I want to conquer it. It's terrific, these houses, yellow in the sun, and the incomparable freshness of the blue. And everywhere the ground is yellow too. I shall send you a better drawing than this rough improvised sketch out of my head later on.

The house on the left is pink with green shutters, I mean the one in the shadow of the tree. That is the restaurant where I go for dinner every day. My friend the postman lives at the end of the street on the left, between the two railway bridges. The night café I painted is not in the picture, it is to the left of the restaurant.

Milliet thinks this horrible [page 85], but I need not tell you that when he says he cannot understand anyone amusing himself doing such a dull grocer's shop, and such stark, stiff houses with no grace whatever, remember that Zola did a certain boulevard at the beginning of L'Assommoir, and Flaubert a corner of the Quai de la Villette in the midst of the dog days at the beginning of Bouvard et Pécuchet and neither of them is mouldy yet.

And it does me good to do difficult things. That does not prevent me from having a terrible need of – shall I say the

Sketch for *Starry Night*

Drawn 1888
Vincent van Gogh Foundation,
Vincent van Gogh Museum, Amsterdam

word? – of religion. Then I go out at night to paint the stars, and I am always dreaming of a picture like this with a group of living figures of our comrades . . .

I should not be surprised if you liked the 'Starry Night' and the 'Ploughed Fields', there is a greater quiet about them than in the other canvases. If the work always went on like that, I should be less worried about money, for it would be easier for people to take to them, if the technique kept on growing more harmonious. But this blasted mistral makes it very hard to get one's brushwork firm and interwoven with feeling, like a piece of music played with emotion . . .

Letter 560, Arles, November 1888

In mid-October Gauguin arrived, and the two artists were soon living the communal life that Vincent had envisaged:

My dear Theo,
It's rather more than time for me too to write you a collected letter for once. First of all let me thank you for your kind letter, also for the 100 franc note it contained. Our days pass in working, working all the time, in the evening we are dead beat and go off to the café, and after that, early to bed! Such is our life.

Of course it's winter here with us too, though it's still very fine from time to time. But I do not dislike trying to work from imagination, since that allows me to stay in. It does not worry me to work in the heat of a stove, but cold does not suit me, as you know . . .

But I have made portraits of a whole family, that of the postman [Joseph Roulin] whose head I had done previously – the man [page 77], his wife [page 93], the baby, the little boy, and the son of sixteen, all characters and very French, though the first has the look of a Russian. Size 15 canvases . . . I hope to get on with this and to be able to get more careful posing, paid for by portraits. And if I manage to do this whole family better still, at least I shall have done something to my liking and something individual . . .

Portrait of Armand Roulin

Painted 1888
66 × 55 cm
Folkwang Museum, Essen

Letter 591, St Rémy, May 1889

After the outbreak of mental illness which brought an end to the experiment with Gauguin, Vincent retired to the asylum at St Rémy. There he gradually took up painting again, and wrote to Theo:

. . .

I wanted to tell you that I think I have done well to come here; first of all, by seeing the reality of the life of various madmen and lunatics in the menagerie, I am losing the vague dread, the fear of the thing. Little by little I can come to look upon madness as a disease like any other . . .

Have you received the case of pictures [from Arles]? I am anxious to know whether or not they have suffered.

I am working on two others – some violet irises and a lilac bush, two subjects taken from the garden.·

The idea of work as a duty is coming back to me very strongly, and I think that all my faculties for work will come back to me fairly quickly. Only work often absorbs me so much that I think I shall always remain absent-minded and awkward in shifting for myself for the rest of my life too . . .

Irises

Painted 1889
71 × 93 cm
J. Paul Getty Museum, Malibu, California

Letter 604, St Rémy, September 1889

The artist found solace in his work and in it sought a respite from the attacks of mental illness. By September, he was looking forward to returning to northern France:

My dear brother,

. . .

I am writing this letter little by little in the intervals when I am tired of painting. Work is going pretty well – I am struggling with a canvas begun some days before my indisposition, a 'Reaper'; the study is all yellow, terribly thickly painted, but the subject was fine and simple. For I see in this reaper – a vague figure fighting like a devil in the midst of the heat to get to the end of his task – I see in him the image of death, in the sense that humanity might be the wheat he is reaping. So it is – if you like – the opposite of the sower I tried to do before. But there's nothing sad in this death, it goes its way in broad daylight with a sun flooding everything with a light of pure gold . . .

. . . I am working like one actually possessed, more than ever I am in a dumb fury of work. And I think that this will help cure me. Perhaps something will happen to me like that of which Eug. Delacroix spoke, 'I discovered painting when I no longer had any teeth or breath left', in the sense that my distressing illness makes me work with a dumb fury – very slowly – but from morning to night without slackening – and – the secret is probably this – work long and slowly . . .

I will go on working very hard and then we shall see if the attack returns about Christmas, and that over, I can see nothing to stop my telling the management here to go to blazes, and returning to the North for a longer or shorter time . . .

There! The 'Reaper' is finished. I think it will be one of those you keep at home – it is an image of death as the great book of nature speaks it – but what I have sought is the 'almost smiling'. It is all yellow, except for a line of violet hills, a pale fair yellow. I find it queer that I saw it like this from between the iron bars of a cell . . .

Enclosed Field with Reaper at Sunrise

Painted 1889
59.5 × 73 cm
Folkwang Museum, Essen

1853 🐦 1890

Vincent

THE PLATES

The potato fields of Drenthe on a dour autumn day.

Van Gogh left The Hague in September 1883, having failed to achieve any sort of lasting domesticity with Sien. She had reverted to prostitution.

'How much sadness there is in life, but one must not, after all, grow melancholy and must look elsewhere, and working is the right thing.'

He drew dark, low-lying farmhouses awaiting winter, a barge being loaded with peat, a man dragging a harrow through heavy soil in preparation for sowing. ('I am ploughing on my canvas as they do on their fields.')

Desperate for companionship, and for someone to follow his example, he urged his brother Theo to give up art dealing and become a painter himself. That, of course, would have meant destitution for them both. He eventually conceded that this would be so but protested 'I would not want to bloom if that meant you had to shrivel; I would not want to develop the artist in me if you had to repress the artist in you for my sake'.

Patting the small bonfire with his spade, the peasant clearing the ground momentarily becomes a devotee, tending the flame.

Peasant Burning Weeds

Painted 1883
30.5 × 39.5 cm
Rijksmuseum Kröller-Müller, Otterlo

'I have tried to emphasize that those people eating their potatoes in the lamplight have dug the earth with those very hands they put into the dish and so it speaks of *manual labour* and how they have honestly earned their food.'

The pastor's son discovers, in a humble meal, vestiges of the Last Supper. The clock ticks beside the Crucifixion on the wall, the dish is shared, the cups are filled and passed round, the lamp burns. The De Groots are a holy family.

Van Gogh spent much of the winter of 1885 considering and rehearsing this, his largest composition, making studies of hands outstretched to give and receive and of the four principal figures, gnarled yet bright-eyed. 'It might very well seem to be a *genuine peasant* painting,' he declared. He was insistent on this: 'When I call myself a peasant painter, it's a real fact.' Combining the emphatic qualities of the style of illustration he so admired in periodicals like *The Graphic* with the robust characteristics of Dutch low-life genre he put together a scene in which all is resolved. They are what they eat, so to speak. 'The colour they are painted in now is like the colour of a very dusty potato, unpeeled of course.' There's a rootedness, a sense of family security glimpsed through a window, an air of sufficiency and content-ment that he both identified with and envied.

The Potato Eaters

Painted 1885
82 × 114 cm
Vincent van Gogh Foundation,
Vincent van Gogh Museum, Amsterdam

On 26 March 1885 Pastor Theodorus van Gogh of the Dutch Reformed Church in Nuenen died of a heart attack on his own doorstep. 'The first impact wasn't so much the shock of it as its gravity', Vincent wrote to his brother. 'Life is not long for anyone and the only thing that matters is what you do with it.'

The old church tower at Nuenen was a landmark, regarded by van Gogh as the fixed point on the local horizon, whether glimpsed through the window of a weaver's cottage or seen all alone, in summer guarding the harvest fields, in winter capped with snow. For forty years it had been awaiting demolition.

In May 1885 the spire was removed. Van Gogh drew the crowd of busybodies at an informal auction of slates and other lumber, including the great iron cross. Much the same crowd as attended Courbet's *Burial at Ornans*, this time picking over the remains of the Catholic church itself.

Van Gogh decided to call his painting of the scene once the crowd had dispersed not *The Old Tower*, say, but *Peasant Cemetery*. 'That ruin tells me how a faith and a religion have mouldered away – strongly founded though they were – and how the life and death of peasant-folk remains forever the same, budding and withering like the grass and the flowers growing there.'

Weeds on the buttresses, belfry shutters askew, crows circling, door gaping: the stronghold of former certainties (Father Church, so to speak) stands derelict. The tower was finally pulled down in 1888.

'I wanted to express what a simple thing death and burial is, as simple as the falling of an autumn leaf – just a bit of earth turned over – a little wooden cross.'

Peasant Cemetery

Painted 1885
63 × 79 cm
Vincent van Gogh Foundation,
Vincent van Gogh Museum, Amsterdam

The family Bible lies open at the Book of Isaiah. Illegibly so, but the double-column brushwork is worthy of Frans Hals, whose example encouraged van Gogh in the belief that black was not to be despised by true colourists. Hals, he reckoned, achieved at least twenty-seven varieties of black.

In this still life, put together six months after his father's death and painted 'in a rush, in one day', the blackness is fuggy, suggesting an all-night vigil before the candle was snuffed out. The Bible on its reading-stand speaks the language the pastor best understood. Isaiah, chapter 53, verse 3: 'He is despised and rejected of men: a man of sorrows and acquainted with grief.' The thumbed yellow-back novel – Zola's relentlessly pessimistic *La Joie de Vivre* – Vincent's rejoinder: Isaiah for modern times.

A strained if not barren relationship is here confessed. The father had been exasperated and distressed by the son's extreme behaviour, slumming among the miners of the Borinage, identifying with the poorest, living with a prostitute, outraging parishioners, refusing to eat properly.

What could Vincent say? 'One starts with a hopeless struggle to follow nature, and everything goes wrong; one ends by calmly creating from one's palette, and nature agrees with it and follows.'

In the autumn of 1885 his mother and youngest brother and sister prepared to leave the parsonage. Vincent himself, with lodgings elsewhere in Nuenen, was penniless. He collected birds' nests, keeping dozens in a cupboard. 'I shall do some drawings on the theme of nests and the birds in their nests inhabited by man, the huts on the heath and their inhabitants,' he told Theo. The severity of *Still Life with Open Bible* (the rectangular pages, the sharp white margins) contrasts with the humble nests, each so homely, each held in a confusion of twigs, each firmly lodged in a broken branch.

Still Life with Open Bible, Candlestick and Novel

Painted 1885
63 × 78 cm
Vincent van Gogh Foundation,
Vincent van Gogh Museum, Amsterdam

'There is – I believe – a school of impressionists. But I don't know much about them' (Letter to Theo, April 1885).

In 1885 van Gogh's allegiance was still to 'Delacroix, Millet, Corot and the rest'. A year later his outlook shifted. Having spent three months in Antwerp, dedicated to life-study, admiring Rubens, diverted by Japanese prints, he moved to Paris in March 1886. Impressionism slowly affected him. There was a relaxation of symbolic intent, a lightening of the palette, a growing awareness of what could be achieved without impasto.

Living in Montmartre with Theo, he took to painting 'the huts on the heath and their inhabitants': the suburban perimeter with windmills on the skyline, quarries and fortifications below and beyond, a shanty area where a peasant way of life held out against urban and industrial development.

Le Moulin de Blute-Fin, Montmartre, painted towards the end of 1886, is more Corot than Pissarro. There is, as yet, no evidence of his 'trying to render intense colour and not a grey harmony'. The tricolour flies on the windmill and van Gogh is doubtless reminded of the carpenter's yard seen from his window in The Hague as he fills in the details of each allotment.

Le Moulin de Blute-Fin, Montmartre

Painted 1886
45.4 × 47.5 cm
Glasgow Art Gallery and Museum

'I have an idea for a kind of signboard, which I hope to carry out', van Gogh wrote in February 1886. 'I mean, for instance, for a fishmonger, still life of fish, for flowers, for vegetables.' The idea was to promote the still life – indoors painting – to a more public domain.

A year later, living with Theo at 54 rue Lepic, van Gogh painted a number of still lives of items close to hand: a clutch of novels, a pot of chives, herrings, a carafe and lemons and, twice over, this basket of sprouting bulbs. Contained within the oval, snug as fledglings in a nest, they give promise of Impressionist stirrings in technique while anticipating spring.

A Basket of Bulbs

Painted 1887
31.5 × 48 cm
Vincent van Gogh Foundation,
Vincent van Gogh Museum, Amsterdam

Van Gogh painted shoes in 1887 because they were there: up to three pairs at a time. Like Sherlock Holmes (whose first published case, *A Study in Scarlet* appeared in *Beeton's Christmas Annual* for 1887), van Gogh read character from footwear. The boot unlaced, its tongue lolling here abuts its companion, upside down with the hobnails glinting.

The motif bears some relation to Theo and Vincent but it is, primarily, a representation of Vincent himself. 'An awkward customer', as a neighbour in one of the apartments at 54 rue Lepic remembered him. Van Gogh believed in walking; he had walked from Ramsgate to Welwyn via London to see his sister; he had tramped the roads of Drenthe; he regarded himself as a pilgrim painter, roughshod and undeviating. There may also be the implication that, as one shoe is useless without the other, so too are he and Theo inseparable.

A Pair of Shoes

Painted 1887
34 × 41.5 cm
Baltimore Museum of Art

Part of van Gogh's intention, on moving to Paris, had been to study at life-drawing classes and to draw from the antique, that is, from plaster casts. The skull was part of the repertoire. In Antwerp he had painted a skeleton, on one occasion with a lit cigarette stuck between its teeth. Here, in one of two studies, the skull is presented as a *contre-jour* death's-head.

Like his nests, his bulbs in a basket and, indeed, any one of his self-portraits, this skull serves as a sign. 'They persist nowadays in believing that *life is flat* and runs from birth to death', he wrote to Emile Bernard in June 1888. 'However life is probably round . . .' The skull, the traditional *memento mori* used by artists down the ages to show the sitter's awareness that portraiture is vanity, grits its teeth and stares blankly.

After leaving Antwerp the twenty-five judges of student work there agreed that van Gogh's work was so crude and inept it qualified only for the eight- to ten-year-old class. The skull may be regarded as a challenge: van Gogh's sign, exercise-book size, that he now knew the virtue of directness. Placed in the category of (innocent) beginner he found himself capable of staring back at the life class. Pears, bulbs, potatoes, boots, books, skulls: he now had the formal ability to treat them as one.

Skull

Painted 1887/8
41.5 × 31.5 cm
Vincent van Gogh Foundation,
Vincent van Gogh Museum, Amsterdam

Painted in the late summer of 1887 in his newly assimilated Impressionist style, thoroughly up-to-date with its sketchiness worthy of Toulouse-Lautrec (who was instrumental in getting him to move south the following year) and its tentative pointillism. The touches of red around the eyes and streaking from the mouth into the beard came from van Gogh's study of Rubens. The hat, a colour essay in itself, fits him like a halo.

'It is a pity that as one gradually gains experience, one gradually loses one's youth.'

Self-Portrait with Straw Hat

Painted 1887
41 × 33 cm
Vincent van Gogh Foundation,
Vincent van Gogh Museum, Amsterdam

Van Gogh had already painted the dealer and colourman Père Tanguy a year before. Now, not long before he left Paris, he painted him again twice. This version, bought by Rodin from Tanguy's daughter, was painted as a form of payment. But it is an affectionate homage to '*si drôle de bon-homme*' – 'such a funny fellow' – with every part of the picture animated in the latest styles: pointillism, of sorts, for the trousers, blues on blue for the jacket, and a background of transcribed Japanese prints.

With his flattened straw hat and narrowed eyes Père Tanguy is become somewhat Japanese himself. He merges with the ground where Mount Fuji, cherry blossom, snows and geisha, irises, streams and flowered meadows serve as van Gogh's travel brochure. Somewhere, well away from Paris where, he declared to Gauguin, he found himself 'very miserable, quite ill, and almost addicted to drink', was a land where a painter could flourish.

'If I can live long enough', he wrote from Arles six months or so later, 'I shall be something like old Tanguy.' When he left Paris, Emile Bernard recalled, he covered the walls of the room he had painted in with Japanese prints. He told Bernard that this was to reassure Theo (who had become distracted by his garrulous, obsessive behaviour). As in the portraits of Père Tanguy, the walls were covered 'in such a way that my brother will think I am still here'.

Portrait of Père Tanguy

Painted 1887–8
92 × 75 cm
Musée Rodin, Paris

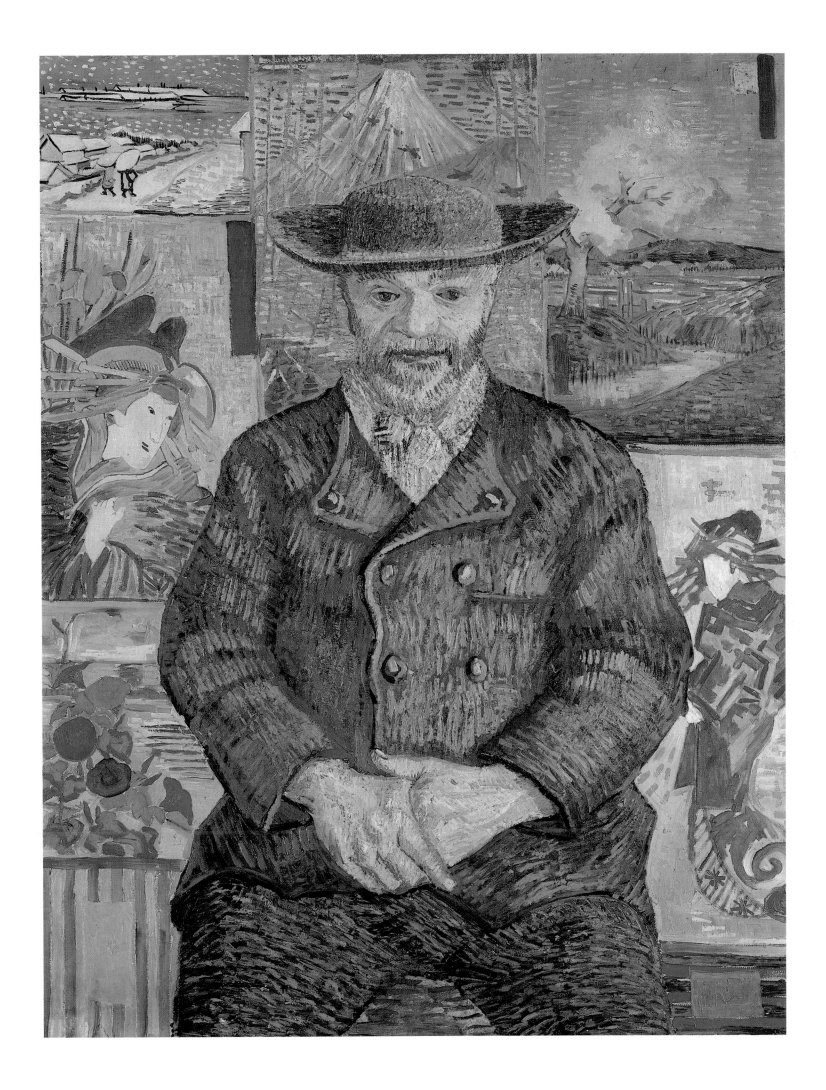

Arriving in Arles on 20 February 1888, van Gogh found deep snow ('really like the winter landscapes of the Japanese') turning to slush and a complete lack of the colourfulness he had expected. He felt stranded. 'The Museum's atrocious: an absolute joke.' There was a lack of people or things to reassure him. His first paintings, a landscape or two and still lives (clogs, potatoes), were little more than exercises to help get him accustomed.

However, two small studies of a blossoming almond twig were a sign though of an unfolding to come. One, with a book placed on the table behind it, he sent to his sister Wil. The other, being uncluttered, was his frontispiece painting for Arles. Like a Manet flower study, it is a painting without complications. It has the simplicity van Gogh associated with Japanese culture. It is a sudden display of virtuosity.

The blue streaks of shadow on yellow ground, the vermilion line on the wall, the green and brown twists of the branch and the fatty outbursts of the buds show what was to become the great characteristic of his art: van Gogh's unerring touch when mood, circumstances, idea and available paint spontaneously combined.

Blossoming Almond in a Glass

Painted 1888
24 × 19 cm
Vincent van Gogh Foundation,
Vincent van Gogh Museum, Amsterdam

'A meadow full of very yellow buttercups, a ditch with irises, green leaves and purple flowers, the town in the background, some grey willows and a strip of blue sky.'

In his letters to Theo, in the sketches he scribbled between lines, and the drawings done as often after as before the main painting, van Gogh staked his position. Each view that he discovered, as spring advanced, became a revelation. There was the sudden abundance of challenges to 'grey harmony', a rival to the old church tower of Nuenen. Orange pantiles instead of slates or thatch, 'that sea of gold with a band of purple irises': the language grew more exultant as his technique sprang into rapid service, the sky laid on thickly so as to counterbalance the serried meadow, the irises snapping open.

'Not a single flower is drawn completely so that they are mere dabs of colour, red, yellow, orange, green, blue, violet, but the impression of all these colours in their juxtaposition is there all right, in the painting as in nature.'

Van Gogh's admiration for John Constable, for a landscape art, Dutch-bred, that gave equal weight to ditch and vista, is hinted at in this painting. The willows grow where once he would have put peasants. Now 'in the painting as in nature', there is no need to follow Millet too closely. Symbolic intent has no place in 'a Provençal orchard of *outstanding gaiety*'.

Field with Flowers

Painted 1888
54 × 65 cm
Vincent van Gogh Foundation,
Vincent van Gogh Museum, Amsterdam

'I have a new subject in hand, fields green and yellow as far as the eye can see . . . It is exactly like a Solomon Konink, you know.'

He meant Philips de Koninck (1619–88), whose speciality was flat land, pale sea and vast clouded skies put together as much from the imagination as from topography. The Crau, five kilometres outside Arles, painted in June as harvesting began, is a busy landscape. Montmajour sits on the far side, in strategic control of the plain, overlooking the railway that van Gogh was to draw a month later. The farms are positioned like blockhouses, each surrounded by many yellows.

The wheel of the blue cart is the hub of the cycle of seasons. Under a sky so cloudless that it looks unchangeable, van Gogh has established a complex account of reaping, carting, stacking and storing: the wide view from a vantage point beside an old mill.

Harvest Landscape

Painted 1888
72.5 × 92 cm
Vincent van Gogh Foundation,
Vincent van Gogh Museum, Amsterdam

Placing himself by a pair of iron gates (that appear in other paintings of this farm) van Gogh must have suddenly seen, in these upside-down nests, the makings of an outsize still life. The stacks crowned with cohesive thatch, with ladders leaning against them like crutches, are unstable in a farmyard dotted and streaked with weeds. The woman with a pail leans towards them, adding to the impression of a task finished in haste.

Enclosing a drawing in a letter to Theo, van Gogh wrote: 'The one with the stacks in the farmyard will appear too eccentric to you, but it was done in a great hurry, by way of a draft for a painting.' The painting has a masterly impatience – hardly any time to establish the trees or add chickens to the stubble. In his haste van Gogh surpassed himself. 'I must warn you that everyone will think that I work too fast. Don't you believe a word of it.'

Haystacks Near a Farm

Painted 1888
73 × 92.5 cm
Rijksmuseum Kröller-Müller, Otterlo

'I imagine the man I have to paint, terrible in the furnace of the heat of harvest-time, as surrounded by the whole Midi.'

Seedtime and harvest, beginning and end, are combined in an image of transcendent energy. Drawings setting out van Gogh's ideas for the painting suggest that the sower is walking a sea such as he had recently seen and drawn at Les Saintes-Maries-de-la-Mer. The stubble is burnished, the sun flowers rather than setting and the standing corn choruses and watches as the crows peck at the fallen seed.

More and more it seems to me that the pictures which must be made so that painting should be wholly itself, and should raise itself to a height equivalent to the serene summits which the Greek sculptors or the German musicians, the writers of French novels reached, are beyond the power of an isolated individual: so they will probably be created by groups of men combining to execute an idea held in common.

Van Gogh repeatedly voiced his hopes for a co-operative sort of art. He had suggested to Theo that he should join him as a painter, he had hopes of working in collaboration or commune with anyone who would agree: Gauguin, perhaps Emile Bernard, even perhaps Toulouse-Lautrec. In *The Sower* he takes a Millet and transforms it; he reaps Impressionism, harvests pointillism, advances his concept of the artist as provider, striding along with the sun at his shoulder. Such composite inspiration was, he felt, somewhat Japanese. 'One's sight changes; you see things with an eye more Japanese. You feel colours differently. The Japanese draw quickly, very quickly, like a lightning flash, because their nerves are finer, their feeling simpler.'

To be Japanese, van Gogh was assuming, was to be like himself. The seasons merge, dawn and sunset, orient and occident, and, convinced that all arts combine, he wrote in June 1888, 'I am reading a book on Wagner. What an Artist. One like that in painting would be something. *It will come.*'

Sower with Setting Sun

Painted 1888
64 × 80.5 cm
Rijksmuseum Kröller-Müller, Otterlo

'A mousme is a Japanese girl – Provençal in this case – twelve to fourteen years old.'

Van Gogh was preoccupied with the painting for a week in July 1888. Apart from an off-duty Zouave, the girl was his first sitter for months. He gave her oleander to hold. 'The oleander – Ah! that speaks of love and is beautiful like the Lesbos of Puvis de Chavannes, with women on the seashore.' Alert but modest she sits, not an intimate and no threat: a Provençale unaware that she is being made to substitute for some imagined Oriental.

Mousme Sitting in a Cane Chair, Half-Figure

Painted 1888
74 × 60 cm
National Gallery of Art, Washington DC

'Lets talk about Frans Hals', van Gogh wrote to Emile Bernard at the time he painted Joseph Roulin, the Arles postal official, for the first time. 'Hammer into your head that master Frans Hals, that painter of all kinds of portraits, of a whole, gallant, live immortal republic.'

Roulin, seated in the same chair as the mousme, became a vital source of support for van Gogh a few months later. 'A head somewhat like Socrates, hardly any nose at all, a high forehead, bald crown, little grey eyes, bright red chubby cheeks, a big pepper-and-salt beard, large ears. This man is an ardent republican and socialist, reasons quite well and knows a lot of things.'

Truculent, still astonished perhaps at being asked to pose ('the good fellow, unwilling as he was to accept money, *cost me more* in food and drink') is a Hals figure in modern dress. There's no Hals finesse in the clumsy uniform, the quick scrawl of frogging on the sleeves. 'To paint in one rush, as much as possible in one rush. What a joy to see such a Frans Hals . . . ' 'I use colour in a more arbitrary way to express myself forcefully.' Joseph Roulin has an expansive complexion, a beard that leaps off the face. His buttons are dabs, his fingers have a life of their own. 'What impassions me most' van Gogh wrote to his sister Wilhelmien, 'is the portrait, the modern portrait.'

Joseph Roulin, Sitting in a Cane Chair, Three-Quarter Length

Painted 1888
81 × 65 cm
Museum of Fine Art, Boston

'In my picture of the "Night Café" I have tried to express the idea that the café is a place where one can ruin oneself, go mad or commit a crime.'

The Café de l'Alcazar, where van Gogh lodged from April to September 1888 while aiming to move into the Yellow House, is represented as a waiting-room for the shiftless, the antechamber to despair.

'It is the equivalent, though different, of *The Potato Eaters*' (page 47). Where the De Groots had been cosily lumped together, like birds in a nest, here solitary men are slumped. At a corner table a whore sits over a drink with her pimp. The chairs pushed back denote those who had homes to go to.

'To the great joy of the landlord, of the postman whom I had already painted, of the visiting night prowlers and of myself, for three nights running I sat up to paint and went to bed during the day.'

The joy has been painted out. Buzzing with sleeplessness the lamps halate, the yellow floorboards raked with sulphur seem barely contained by the stifling red and green of the walls. The billiard table stands like a bier in front of the bottle altar beneath the midnight clock.

'The picture is one of the ugliest I have done.'

The Night Café

Painted 1888
70 × 89 cm
Yale University Art Gallery

Legend has it that van Gogh stuck candles on his hat in order to see clearly enough to paint outdoors at night here in the Place du Forum and beside the Rhône. An image of the artist with a burning crown lurking in the shadows therefore attaches to this painting. But as he explained, 'an immensely large streetlamp illuminates the terrace, the façade, the pavement'.

Whatever the precise set-up, when he produced this painting, in September 1888, he wrote self-depracatingly to Gauguin about what he was accomplishing. 'A sincerity, perhaps original at times, in what I feel, if only the subject can lend something to my rash and clumsy execution.'

Café Terrace is audaciously original in its succinct account of different qualities of light. The café lamp is the melting focus of the picture. It casts discs on the tables, floods wall and awning and sprinkles the cobbles with gold. Waiter and strollers are caught by it and the inner light of the café is made secondary, a cooler yellow. While the stars flare and silver the upper storeys, a carriage lamp and lit windows mark the darkness dividing the immediate from the eternal.

'The problem of painting night scenes or effects, on the spot and actually by night interests me tremendously', he wrote on 17 September. With highlights and silhouettes dancing from the empty chairs at the edge of the terrace to where he sat, van Gogh brilliantly resolved a formal problem.

Café Terrace at Night

Painted 1888
81 × 65.5 cm
Rijksmuseum Kröller-Müller, Otterlo

Having rented the Yellow House in May, van Gogh waited all summer before moving in: he hadn't the money to make it habitable until he received a small legacy from an uncle, enough to buy some chairs and other furniture. In August, anticipating Gauguin's arrival to share the house, he painted his first *Sunflowers*.

'Yellow is the embodiment of the utmost clarity of Love.' He intended a symphonic effect. 'Raw or broken chrome yellows will blaze forth on various backgrounds.' The sunflowers would furnish the small rooms, and they would produce 'the same kind of effect as Gothic church windows'.

With a rapidity worthy of Frans Hals, with a succulence, when still freshly painted, that must have made them glare on the pale blue walls, the sunflowers were a decorative scheme that represented van Gogh's idea of 'an association of painters'. They were supposed to cast a benign glow over the work he and Gauguin would undertake. As he admitted a year later, 'to attain the high yellow note that I attained last summer I really had to be pretty well keyed up'.

Fourteen Sunflowers in a Vase

Painted 1888
93 × 73 cm
National Gallery, London

'I want to paint men and women with something of the eternal which the halo used to symbolize', van Gogh wrote in August 1888. The following month he painted Second Lieutenant Milliet of the Zouaves, himself an amateur painter who went sketching with him to Montmajour. Years later Milliet recalled 'he painted too big, he didn't pay any attention to details, he didn't draw, you know'. He found van Gogh 'very nervous'.

'The red kepi against an emerald-green background': instead of the halo there was the regimental insignia of moon and stars. Lieutenant Milliet wears a medal awarded for military service in Tonkin: he had gone East and, however prosaic his outlook, he represented, to van Gogh, a connection with the Exotic.

'A fine subject.'

Lieutenant Milliet

Painted 1888
60 × 49 cm
Rijksmuseum Kröller-Müller, Otterlo

Gauguin arrived in Arles on 23 October. The Alyscamps ('Elysian Fields'), the Roman cemetery in the town, became a subject for both of them, a test of compatibility.

Gauguin treated the poplars and sarcophagi, ranged along an avenue, like anywhere else, outlining masses and filling them in thinly, exaggerating the autumn colours with his Symbolist palette. Van Gogh, encouraged by Gauguin to think badly of his whole approach, his 'rash and clumsy execution', created two banal and two dramatically formalized Alyscamps scenes.

'It is some poplar trunks cut by the frame where the leaves begin.' Between the trees the sarcophagi are lined up in perspective (outdoor versions of the billiard table in the Café de l'Alcazar) and the promenading figures are elongated in a Japanese manner.

Gauguin and van Gogh went to Montpellier together and saw Courbet's *Bonjour, Monsieur Courbet* in the museum there. They also went on what Gauguin described as 'nocturnal promenades for reasons of hygiene' to the Maison Tutelle and other brothels. 'With Gauguin blood and sex prevail over ambition', van Gogh wrote soon after Gauguin's arrival. In the Alyscamps he proved himself the one who appreciated the long, historical perspective of the place. Gauguin, in Arles on sufferance, painted like a tourist.

Les Alyscamps

Painted 1888
73 × 92 cm
Rijksmuseum Kröller-Müller, Otterlo

The chair is the man. Van Gogh had long thought so. He had been impressed by Luke Fildes' drawing (published in the Christmas 1870 number of *The Graphic*) showing Dickens' study immediately after he died, the writer's paraphernalia neatly laid out on the desk, the chair pushed aside.

It was 'quite amusing' he remarked, to portray character through the chair. By December 1888 relations with Gauguin were strained. 'Our arguments are terribly electric, sometimes we come out of them with our heads as exhausted as a used electric battery.' In some circumstances they were at opposite poles: van Gogh saw himself by daylight, a plain peasant chair planted firmly on the floor, onions in a box behind. Very open. 'I tried for an effect of light by means of direct colour.'

The pipe and tobacco pouch were van Gogh's usual attributes, though in this instance ('quite amusing') it is possible that the double-meaning of *'blague'* or tobacco pouch has a bearing on it. *'Blague'* is slang for nonsense. Though never one to ridicule himself, here van Gogh is representing himself, compared to Gauguin, as guileless and uncomplicated. The bluff one. 'In any case', he wrote 'I must beware of my nerves.'

Vincent's Chair

Painted 1888
93 × 73.5 cm
National Gallery, London

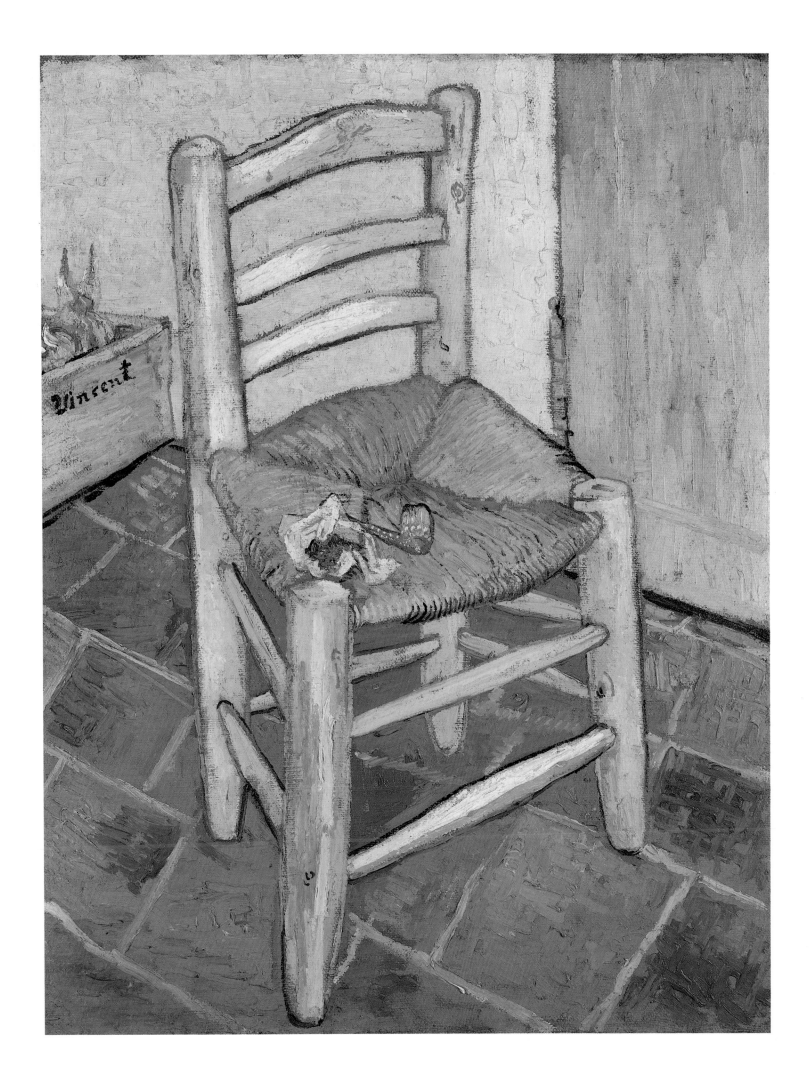

Curving in all directions, with grasping arms and aggressive legs, this is the chair of a vehement man, the chair assigned to him by van Gogh.

It basks in artificial light, the candle flame flaring sideways, the lamp on the wall more symbolic than actual. The restless, sarcastic Gauguin, full of ideas, braces himself. He was considering leaving. 'Vincent and I simply cannot live together in peace because of incompatability of temper.'

'Gauguin gives me the courage to imagine things and certainly things from the imagination take on a more mysterious character,' van Gogh wrote at the beginning of December. Then, on 23 December he wrote to Theo: 'Gauguin is very powerful, strongly creative, but just because of that he must have peace. Will he find it anywhere if he does not find it here? I am waiting for him to make a decision with absolute serenity.'

Within hours van Gogh mutilated himself by cutting off the lobe of his left ear. The *Forum Republican*, Journal of the Arrondissement of Arles, reported:

Last Sunday at 11.30 pm, one Vincent Vaugogh [sic], painter, of Dutch origin, presented himself at the maison de tolerance No.1, asked for one Rachel and gave her ... his ear saying 'Look after this object carefully'. Then he disappeared.

Gauguin's Chair
Painted 1888
90.5 × 72 cm
Vincent van Gogh Foundation,
Vincent van Gogh Museum, Amsterdam

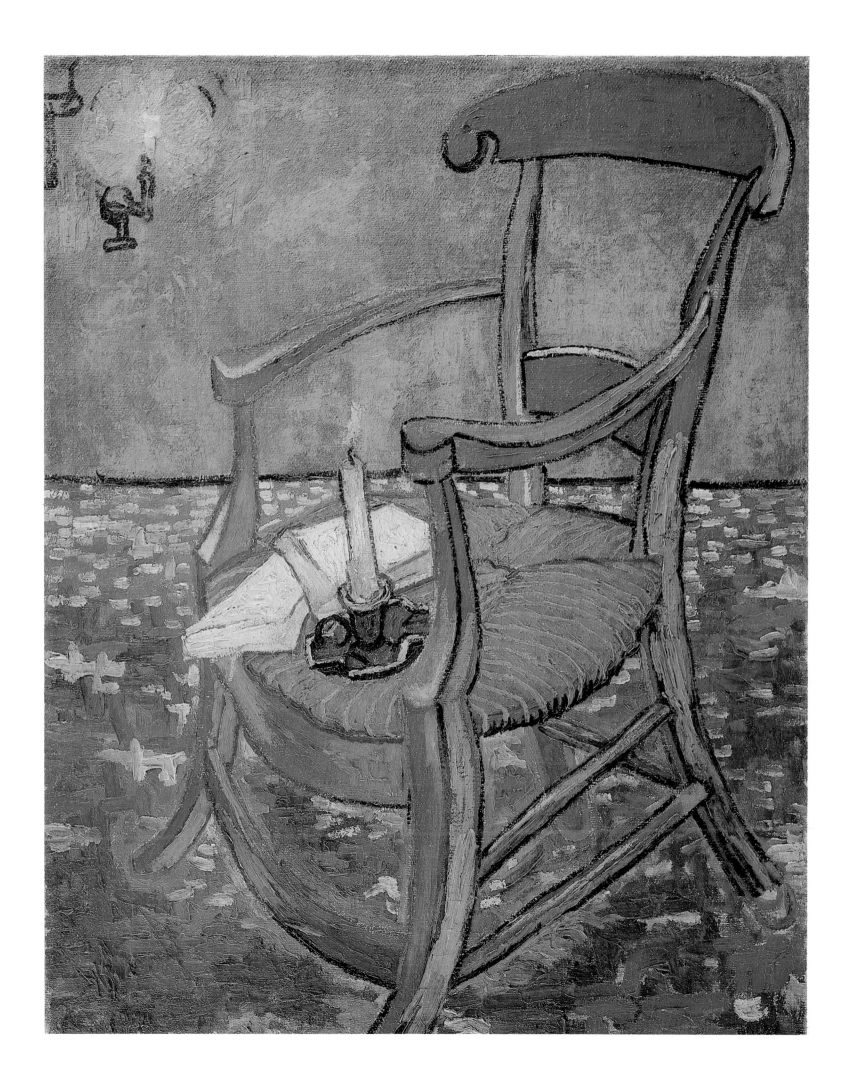

Five times over – creating a lullaby for himself – van Gogh painted the same reassuring portrait of the wife of Roulin, the jovial post office official who helped him home after the incident at the brothel and gave him much support in the subsequent weeks.

Madame Roulin sits in what could be Gauguin's chair, watching over the unseen cradle. Roulin himself and Dr Felix Rey of the Arles hospital were also painted against the busy wallpaper but it was she to whom van Gogh kept returning. He thought of the composition as the centrepiece of a triptych, with sunflowers on either side.

Writing to Gauguin, in late January, van Gogh said 'As an impressionist arrangement of colours I have never invented anything better. And I believe that if one put this picture, such as is, in a fisherman's boat, even Icelandic fishermen, there would be those who would feel inside there the cradle-song.'

He had conceived *The Sunflowers* (page 83) as radiant, like 'Gothic church windows'. *La Berceuse*, the image of motherhood, was to be the embodiment of loving reassurance, 'the reds going to pure oranges, rising more in the flesh colours as far as the chromes merging into pinks and combining with olives and malachite greens'. *La Berceuse* was, by the fifth time he painted it, van Gogh's final riposte to Gauguin.

Augustine Roulin (La Berceuse)

Painted 1888–9
92 × 73 cm
Rijksmuseum Kröller-Müller, Otterlo

'I am going to begin by doing one or two still lives so as to get back into the habit of painting.' It was the first week of January. Van Gogh had left the hospital and returned to the Yellow House for a few weeks until, in February, a further crisis put him back in hospital.

On the table he laid out what he had. His attributes: onions and tobacco pipe. His candle, still burning, and a spent match beside a 'kind' letter from Theo, whose announcement that he was intending to get married had probably helped precipitate the breakdown before Christmas. The *Manuel Annuaire de la Santé ou Médecine et Pharmacie Domestiques* by F.V. Raspail was a popular medical companion. Remedies recommended by Raspail included onions.

Though a convalescent painting, the still life is as complex as any van Gogh created. He assembles his hopes and flanks them with the empty bottle and the open kettle. Where once he placed his father's Bible now he relies on his own resources, and word from his distant brother.

Still Life with Onions and Book

Painted 1889
50 × 64 cm
Rijksmuseum Kröller-Müller, Otterlo

'During my illness I saw again every room in the house at Zundert, every path, every plant in the garden, the views of the fields outside, the neighbours, the graveyard, the church, our kitchen garden at the back – down to a magpie's nest in a tall acacia in the graveyard.'

The print on the wall of the Yellow House signals still a world of bold lines and strong colours, a world he resignedly turns his back on. 'I am too old and (especially if I have a papier-mâché ear put on) too jerry-built to go there.'

In pose he begins to resemble Père Tanguy, but it is the buttoned-up convalescent, allowed out because he has apparently made a good recovery, who stares so. 'Serenity returns to my brain day by day', he reassured Theo. But he also said 'If I did not have your friendship I should be remorselessly driven to suicide, and, cowardly as I am, I should commit it in the end.'

Self-Portrait with Bandaged Ear

Painted 1889
60 × 49 cm
Courtauld Institute Galleries, London

Writing to the painter Paul Signac, who had visited him in hospital, van Gogh described seeing and painting his second spring in the Crau.

'A poor landscape with little cottages, blue skyline of the Alpine foothills, sky white and blue. The foreground, patches of land surrounded by cane hedges, where small peach trees are in bloom – everything is small there, the gardens, the fields, the orchards, and the trees, even the mountains, as in certain Japanese landscapes, which is the reason why the subject attracted me.'

The view reminiscent of Philips de Koninck has shifted. The blue cart is now on the extreme left and peach trees flourish where previously, it seems, they had been edited out. Celebrating his days of release from hospital, van Gogh aerates the sky with shimmering dots, reminiscent of Signac's pointillism, and flecks the whole picture with the goose-pimples raised by the cold, dry mistral wind.

Soon after this Theo wrote to tell him he had married Johanna Bonger, on 17 April. Another crisis, as a result of which (and of the hostility whipped up in Arles against him) it was decided that van Gogh should go to the Maison de Santé at Saint-Rémy de Provence, near Tarascon.

The Crau with Peach Trees in Bloom

Painted 1889
65.5 × 81.5 cm
Courtauld Institute Galleries, London

Painted from memory, Saint-Rémy. The perspective of *The Night Café* lengthens into another sort of dreariness. Draped beds with labels identifying each patient are substituted for the marble-topped tables, a crucifix hangs in place of the clock.

The hospital had been a refuge from pestering children egged on by hostile adults who got up a petition demanding van Gogh's committal as a madman. The staff had been sympathetic. But there was no privacy, no long-term prospect. At Saint-Rémy, admitted as a third-class inmate 'to prevent a recurrence of previous attacks', he had at least a room of his own, with another available as a studio.

'What you ought to know', Theo wrote, 'is that from one point of view you are not to be pitied, though it may not seem so.'

Dormitory in the Hospital

Painted 1889
74 × 92 cm
Private Collection

Through the bars of his upstairs cell van Gogh could see the Alpilles beyond the cloister garden wall. Omitting the bars he painted the enclosure again and again, showing the wheat growing, ripening, being reaped. He telescoped the hills into mountainous encroachments and set the walls tilting wildly.

The monk and the painter here coincide. 'I have been "in a hole" all my life, and my mental condition is not only vague *now*, but *has always been so*, so that whatever is done for me, I *cannot* think things out so as to balance my life.'

In the asylum, he wrote, 'you continually hear terrible cries and howls like beasts in a menagerie'. He was allowed out, with an escort, into the grounds and the neighbourhood. 'When I am working in the garden they all come to look, and I assure you they have the discretion and manners to leave me alone – more than the good people of the town of Arles, for instance.'

The wall rides the field, flinging itself across, warding off the world beyond where the sun looms more orientally than ever.

Mountain Landscape Seen across the Walls with Rising Sun and Green Field

Painted 1889
72 × 92 cm
Rijksmuseum Kröller-Müller, Otterlo

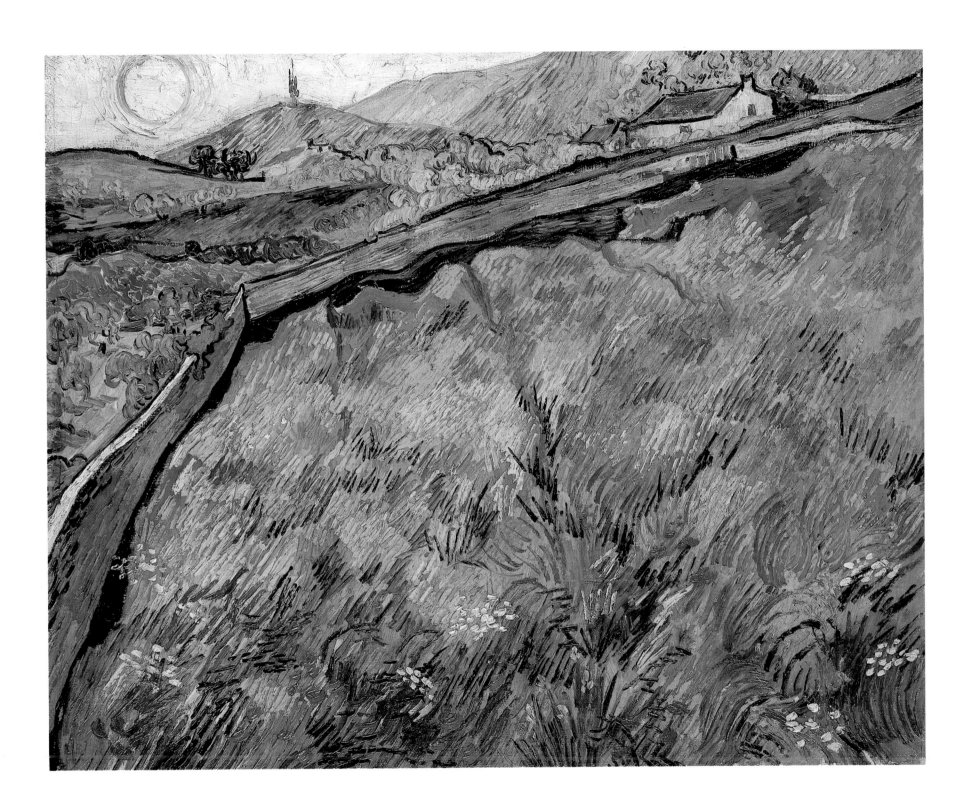

Though the cypresses respond to the agitated sky, the bushes squirm and the wheat ripples, this study of a corner of a field just beyond the cloister walls is a landscape of mood comparable to *Chill October* by the former Pre-Raphaelite John Millais, which van Gogh had seen in 1875.

'I have always remembered some English pictures such as "Chill October",' he wrote in 1884. Where Millais concentrated on the grey harmony of autumn coming on, sedge withering and trees dimming as evening draws in, van Gogh put all his energy into the convulsions of high summer with a mistral blowing: the landscape of the South distantly echoing that of the reticent North.

Wheat Field with Cypresses

Painted 1889
72 × 91 cm
National Gallery, London

'The cypresses are always occupying my thoughts. I should like to make something of them like the canvases of the sunflowers because it astonishes me that they have *not yet been done as I see them.*'

Furious, italicized, the trees join forces with the rampaging night sky. Winds suffused with brimming stars, adorned with Lieutenant Milliet's moon insignia, storm the land.

'Why, I ask myself, shouldn't the shining dots of the sky be as accessible as the black dots on the map of France? Just as we take a train to reach Tarascon or Rouen, we take death to reach a star.'

That summer at Saint-Rémy van Gogh had been reading Shakespeare. Hence, perhaps, 'the floor of heaven . . . thick inlaid with patines of bright gold'. By late June (when he painted *Starry Night*) he was half way, he said, through *Henry V*, reaching the finest rhetoric.

And those that leave their valiant bones in France,
Dying like men, though buried in your dung-hills,
They shall be fam'd; for there the sun shall greet them,
And draw their honours reeking up to heaven.

The bars of the cell have fallen away. The cypresses aspire. 'Under the great starlit vault of heaven something which after all one can only call God.'

Starry Night

Painted 1889
73 × 92 cm
Museum of Modern Art, New York

'This new attack, old chap, seized me on a windy day in the fields when I was in the midst of painting. I finished the canvas nevertheless. I will send it to you.'

Periods of particular lucidity often precede epileptic attacks, and what was true of Dostoevsky appears to have been true of van Gogh. Painting 'day in day out', as he said, 'to avoid being distracted' he drove himself to collapse. The pallor of this self-portrait partly stems from his lack of colours: Prussian blue, chrome yellow and white were his main resort. But there is an intensity stemming from extreme, rapid concentration. 'Work . . . will be the best lightning conductor for my malady.' Not knowing the reason for his affliction (syphilis acquired in Antwerp, perhaps, manic-depressive behaviour brought on by circumstances, some form of epilepsy or inherited instability), van Gogh could only attempt to live through it to some purpose.

The greenish flames belong to the iconography of passion, but for van Gogh they are more immediate: wallpaper grown vibrant, mood turned horrific, something of what he had perceived in the atmosphere of *The Night Café* (page 79): 'an atmosphere like a devil's furnace, of pale sulphur'.

Self-Portrait

Painted 1889
65 × 54 cm
Musée d'Orsay, Paris

In July Jo, his sister-in-law, wrote saying she was pregnant and asking him to be godfather. The news disturbed him. He went to Arles to collect some paintings, saw Rachel the prostitute and returned to Saint-Rémy delirious. 'For many days together I have been *absolutely* distraught as at Arles, quite as badly, if not worse.'

'During my illness a misfortune happened to me – that lithograph of Delacroix, the 'Pietà', fell with some other prints into some oil and paint and was ruined. I was upset about it – so I made myself sit down and paint it.'

Copying was a means of reinvigorating himself. Emboldened in the transcription, suffused once again with colour, van Gogh's Delacroix is a Delacroix reanimated. 'I hope it has feeling', he wrote.

'My mind clear and my fingers so sure of themselves.' Though confined, and seeing other art in print form only, van Gogh found himself retracing what he admired: it was a return to his original passions, the honesty of Millet, the vitality of Delacroix. Copying was both exercise and homage. It also represented van Gogh's striving for a common language in which all would be reconciled, like to like, 'marrying form and colour'.

Pietà (after Delacroix)

Painted 1889
73 × 60.5 cm
Vincent van Gogh Foundation,
Vincent van Gogh Museum Amsterdam

The first version of *The Artist's Bedroom* was painted in October 1888, soon after van Gogh moved into the Yellow House.

'I wanted to achieve an effect of simplicity of the sort one finds in *Felix Holt*. After being told this you may quickly understand the picture.'

George Eliot's *Felix Holt* ends with contentment as Esther resolves to marry the good Felix. For this scene 'Esther chose to sit in the kitchen, in the wicker chair against the white table, between the fire and the window. The kettle was singing and the clock was ticking steadily towards four o'clock.' All's well and security for life is achieved.

In van Gogh's bedroom 'colour is to do everything', he wrote, and 'giving by its simplification a grander style to things, is to be suggestive here of *rest* and sleep in general'.

The two versions done in the autumn of 1889, at Saint-Rémy, have the same essentials: the sturdy bed, the wash-stand, the two chairs. The paintings on the walls alter, but the snugness remains. The room has been opened out like a stage set. Here, demonstrably, lies contentment. His cell at Saint-Rémy had green curtains with roses on, 'relics of some rich and ruined deceased'. Painting 'duplicates for family and friends' of a composition in which he itemized furniture he actually owned, in a house he had regarded as his, was 'comfortable, as music is comforting', he said. 'It does me good and drives away, I think, the abnormal ideas.'

The Artist's Bedroom in Arles

Painted 1889
56.5 × 74 cm
Musée d'Orsay, Paris

The stream runs through cavities in the limestone of the Alpilles at 'Les Peyroulets' ('little saucepans'), a gorge some distance from Saint-Rémy. van Gogh went there with a warder who knew the area.

This is the second version of the landscape, painted in December 1889. Of the ten paintings van Gogh showed the following March at the Société des Artistes Indépendents, *The Ravine* was the one that brought most comment. While Theo told him that Pissarro had mentioned that 'Monet said that your pictures were the best of all in the exhibition', Gauguin wrote saying 'to many artists you are the most remarkable one in the exhibition' and went on to suggest a swap. 'I should like to exchange with you for anything of mine you choose. The one I mean is a mountainous landscape: two very small travellers seem to be climbing in search of the unknown. It's beautiful and impressive. I've talked at length about it with Aurier, Bernard and many others. All congratulate you.'

The Ravine had its impact on the School of Pont-Aven. In van Gogh's œuvre it marks the onset of a particularly turbulent phase. The clumps of scrub flame on the slopes and the stream 'white and foaming like soapsuds', he wrote to his mother, force the pace.

During December, over Christmas, he suffered two attacks and a relapse.

The Ravine

Painted 1889
73 × 92 cm
Rijksmuseum Kröller-Müller, Otterlo

Kept indoors by bad weather and his nervous state, van Gogh painted a number of copies after Daumier, Doré and, particularly, Millet in December and January 1889–90. He worked from engravings, 'translating into another language, the language of colours'.

Noon is Millet, 'the voice of the wheat' rendered cloudless and golden. van Gogh repays previous borrowings: the tousled straw, the pair of shoes and the pair of sickles resting together. From Millet van Gogh had derived his peasantry language, the concentration on moments when labour appears dignified, wholly responsible, diurnal.

This image shows blissful peace after productive hours. The painting preaches basic contentment.

'The *interpretation* of the composer is something, and it is not a hard and fast rule that only the composer should play his own composition.'

Noon: Rest (after Millet)

Painted 1890
73 × 92 cm
Musée d'Orsay, Paris

Taken from one of Gustave Doré's illustrations, engraved by H. Pisan, for his huge volume *London*, 1872.

This is not just Newgate prison but also, clearly, the universal plight of the prisoner, whether convict or asylum inmate. Van Gogh had read an article on Dostoevsky's *Notes from the House of the Dead*: the exercise yard rehearses his thoughts.

'Many people do not copy, many others do — started on it accidentally and I find that it teaches me things, and above all it sometimes gives me consolation.'

The prison walls, coloured by van Gogh, change from grey to yellow as they open to the light. Two butterflies flutter far above the prisoners' heads. Doré's London, which was also van Gogh's London shortly after, was a place of melodramatic contrasts: high life in Richmond or Rotten Row and, over the page, dismal squalor down in the docks or beneath railway arches. The *Prisoners' Round* is the oppressive monotony of a built-up society. The vertical pit-shaft of despair contrasts with the sprawling ease of *Noon: Rest*.

Prisoners' Round (after Doré)

Painted 1890
80 × 64 cm
Pushkin Museum, Moscow

'Today I received your good news that you are at last a father, that the most critical time is over for Jo, and finally that the little boy is well.'

'We shall give him your name', Theo wrote. 'My wish is that he will have the same perseverance and will be just as courageous as you.' He enclosed an article that had appeared in the *Mercure de France*: 'Les Isolés', by Albert Aurier, the first full appreciation of van Gogh to be published, a hectic one to say the least. ('In his categorical affirmation of the essential character of things, in his often rash simplification of form, in his insolent desire to look at the sun face to face, in the passion of his drawing and colour, there lies revealed a powerful one, a male, a darer . . . ')

Van Gogh responded at length to Aurier. 'Many thanks for your article . . . which greatly surprised me. I like it very much as a work of art in itself, in my opinion your words are colourful, in short, I rediscover my canvases in your article, but better than they are, richer, more full of meaning.'

Meanwhile he began a painting celebrating the birth. 'I started straight away making a picture for him, to hang in their bedroom, big branches of white almond blossom against a blue sky,' he told his mother.

This was a painting to be gazed up into, a painting to herald growth and renewal. He probably used cut branches but, unlike the almond twig in a glass, painted in Arles two years before, here the branches take over, crowding in from three sides in family celebration.

In August 1880 he had written to Theo 'you see that I am in a rage of work, though for the moment it doesn't produce very brilliant results. But I hope these thorns will bear their white blossoms in due time, and that this apparently sterile struggle is none other than the labour of childbirth. First pain, then the joy.'

In late February 1890, van Gogh suffered a ten-month breakdown. 'My work was going well,' he wrote in April. 'The last canvas of branches in bloom – you will see that it was perhaps the best, the most patiently worked thing I had done, painted with calm and with a great firmness of touch. And the next day, down like a brute.'

Branches of an Almond Tree in Blossom

Painted 1890
73 × 92 cm
Vincent van Gogh Foundation,
Vincent van Gogh Museum, Amsterdam

On 16 May Dr Peyron noted: 'Today he requests his release to go and live in the north of France, in the hope that the climate will prove more favourable.'

The irises, bursting from the vase in reckless profusion, were part of van Gogh's last minute attempt to embrace the South. 'I saw the country again, fresh and full of flowers after the rain – how many things there were I could still have made.'

Keyed up, anticipating the move, he painted furiously for a fortnight, from early morning until night. 'The brush strokes come like clockwork.' Where he had originally intended his sunflowers to be golden against royal blue, here contrast is reversed and the blooms are haloed.

On meeting him, for the first time, on 17 May in Paris, Jo van Gogh-Bonger was surprised. 'I had expected a sick man, but here was a sturdy, broad-shouldered man, with a healthy colour, a smile on his face and a very resolute appearance.'

Vase with Violet Irises

Painted 1890
92 × 73.5 cm
Metropolitan Museum of Art, New York

Irises, roses, a field with butterflies, a version of Rembrandt's *Raising of Lazarus* and 'finally a "Cypress with a Star" '. The last paintings van Gogh produced in Saint-Rémy were a resumé made urgent by expectation.

Road with Men Walking (Cypress with a Star) is *Starry Night* dying down, the night sky seething less, the cypress calmer, the ground streaming along in the same magnetic field.

'The north will interest me like a new country', van Gogh wrote. 'My wish to leave here now is imperative.' In the painting, under 'a moon lacking radiance', a carriage approaches, overtaking 'two belated pedestrians. Very romantic maybe, but also Provence, I think.'

The Alpilles swing round from the left, the further cypresses, guarding the cottage, put up their protective, four-poster coverage, the road presses on. This is the end of the working day, the close of a period, for van Gogh, of being far removed, communicating – if not by painting – by letter.

Road with Men Walking

Painted 1890
92 × 73 cm
Rijksmuseum Kröller-Müller, Otterlo

The same approach as *Road with Men Walking* (page 125), only here, in Auvers-sur-Oise, not far from Paris, the path divides and the church stands bolder than any cypress.

'It is almost the same thing as the studies I made at Nuenen of the old tower and the churchyard, though now the colour is probably more expressive, more sumptuous.'

Back in the North van Gogh encountered again the dominance of the village church, the lofty belfry, the shouldering aisle roof, the stout buttresses. High summer brings blue and green. 'The building appears purplish against a deep blue sky, of pure cobalt; the stained-glass windows appear like blotches of ultramarine blue, the roof is purple and in part orange. In the foreground some green plants in bloom.'

The Church in Auvers

Painted 1890
94 × 74 cm
Musée d'Orsay, Paris

Dr Paul-Ferdinand Gachet was a specialist in nervous diseases, a believer in homeopathic medicine and an amateur artist. He had lived in Auvers since 1872 and practised three days a week in Paris. Pissarro recommended him to Theo in October 1889: from then on the plan was to establish Vincent where Gachet could kep an eye on him.

The two men hit it off. Van Gogh discovered a pleasing melancholy in Gachet. 'He lost his wife some years ago, which greatly contributes to his being a broken man . . . he is as disorganized about his job as a doctor as I am about my painting.' Warming to him he declared him 'something like another brother, so much do we resemble each other physically and also mentally'.

'A suntanned face the colour of an overheated brick with red hair and a white cap.' Dr Gachet had a printing press and encouraged van Gogh to make etchings. He had him to dinner every Sunday or Monday, showed him his Pissarro and his Cézannes. 'To use the expression "Love of Art" is hardly an exact term' he said. 'It is the word "Belief" that should be used, belief, to the point of martyrdom.'

Van Gogh's sentiments exactly. Sitting for him, Gachet adopted the pose of sympathetic listener holding foxgloves denoting a natural remedy. This is the second version of the portrait. 'M. Gachet is absolutely *fanatical* about this portrait and wants me to do one for him.'

'I should like to paint portraits which would appear after a century to the people living then as apparitions. By which I mean that I do not endeavour to achieve this by photographic resemblance but by means of our impassioned expressions – that is to say, using our knowledge of and our modern taste for colour.'

Doctor Gachet

Painted 1890
68 × 57 cm
Musée d'Orsay, Paris

In the last week of June van Gogh painted this portrait, envisaging it hung next to a horizontal painting of a wheat field. 'We are still far from the time when people will understand the curious relation between one fragment of nature and another which all the same explain each other and enhance each other.'

Dr Gachet's daughter occupies the same size canvas as, for example, *Wheat Field under Threatening Skies* (page 137). She provides musical accompaniment. 'The dress is pink, the wall in the background green with orange dots, the carpet red with green dots, the piano dark violet.' The dots are orchestrated, pushing upwards, swirling through the skirt and peppering the wall.

'A figure I did with pleasure – but difficult.' Marguerite Gachet is absorbed in her pose at the keyboard, a disassociated figure, unlike Gachet who comes close, like a mirror image.

Marguerite Gachet at the Piano

Painted 1890
102 × 50 cm
Kunstmuseum, Basel

'Some fields seen from a height with a road and a little carriage on it.'

Where the blue cart had stood in his paintings of the Crau, where a plough stands in Millet's painting *Winter, the plain of Chantilly* (copied by van Gogh six months before), here the carriage heads one way, the train streaming clouds in the opposite direction. Van Gogh has positioned himself overlooking the fields of both his 'campaign in the South' and his affiliations in the North: Millet, Pissarro and, beyond them, Ruysdael and Philips de Koninck. The glistening wet road, the patches of crops, poppies and walls and tiled roofs put what he had learned around Arles into a fresh light.

Landscape with Carriage and Train in the Distance

Painted 1890
72 × 90 cm
Pushkin Museum, Moscow

In mid-June van Gogh wrote Gauguin a letter he never sent.

'Look, here's an idea may suit you. I am trying to do some studies of wheat like this (but I can't seem to draw it), nothing but ears of wheat with blue-green stalks, long leaves like ribbons of green shot with pink, ears that are just turning yellow, edged with the soft pink of the dusty bloom – a pink bindweed down below twisted round a stem.'

The field of vision entirely filled with growth and abundance. The wheat field at Saint-Rémy tilting up, the butterflies on grass painted just before he left Saint-Rémy, and the almond branches celebrating the birth of his nephew. *Ears of Wheat* ('the soft rustle of the ears as they sway in the breeze') is a culmination: van Gogh at his most direct. The bird's nest, the bulbs, the haystack, the skull, the sunflowers, the head of Joseph Roulin with flowing beard: the wheat field combines them all. Closing in, cropping the image arbitrarily, ignoring distance, in effect eliminating perspective, turning the Japanese ideal and the background rhythms of wallpaper into a kind of chorus ('Millet . . . the voice of the wheat' amplified) van Gogh achieves formal and emotional unison.

'What the germinating force is in the grain of the wheat, *love is in us*' (Paris, 1887).

'What else can one do, when we think of all the things we do not know the reason for, than go to look at a field of wheat? The history of those plants is like our own; for aren't we, who live on bread, to a considerable extent like wheat, at least aren't we forced to submit to growing like a plant without the power to move . . . (Saint-Rémy, 1889)

Ears of Wheat

Painted 1890
64.5 × 47 cm
Vincent van Gogh Foundation,
Vincent van Gogh Museum, Amsterdam

'They are vast stretches of cornfield under troubled skies, and I did not need to go out of my way to try to express sadness and the extreme of loneliness. I hope you will see them soon – for I hope to bring them to you in Paris as soon as possible since I almost think that these canvases will tell you, what I meant to say in words, the *health and strengthening* that I can see in the country.'

This painting, so obviously disturbed, is too easily interpreted as van Gogh's last: a painting in which paths stretch like arms and legs flung across the corn and crows rise, as though alarmed by a gunshot.

But it was painted more than a fortnight before van Gogh borrowed a pistol from his landlord 'to shoot crows'. He had just returned from seeing Theo in Paris. 'Back here I still feel very sad and continue to feel the storm which threatens you weighing on me also. What was to be done – you see I try generally to be fairly cheerful, but my life too is threatened at the very root, and my steps too are wavering.'

In other paintings done at the same time, 'vast spaces of corn after the rains', everything conspires to suggest agoraphobia. The fields lose contact with the ground, the skies bustle incoherently and bunting hangs in front of the Town Hall of Auvers for an unattended Bastille Day. Roots and trees fight one another, a man on a roof struggles with the thatch.

Wheat Field under Threatening Skies

Painted 1890
50.5 × 100.5 cm
Vincent van Gogh Foundation,
Vincent van Gogh Museum, Amsterdam

Auvers in rain, Auvers nestling, roofs tucked among the trees and only the church tower standing out against the hillside. The scene has all the makings of a failed harvest, after Hokusai.

'We do not feel we are dying, but we do feel the truth that we are of small account, and that we are paying a hard price to be a link in the chain of artists, in health, in youth, in liberty, none of which we enjoy' (letter to Theo, May 1888).

Van Gogh lived to see the harvest of 1890 begun, the reaped wheat bundled into stooks, the stubble ready for burning. While the rain lasted, though, he saw only the blurring, the dissolving, the sodden fields lying open like the illegible pages of the family bible (page 51).

For he shall grow up . . . as a tender plant, and as a root out of a dry ground: he hath no form nor comeliness: and when we shall see him there is no beauty that we should desire him.

He is despised and rejected of men: a man of sorrows and acquainted with grief . . . he was despised and we esteemed him not.

Surely he hath borne our griefs, and carried our sorrows: yet we did esteem him stricken, smitten of God and afflicted.

Isaiah Chapter 53

At the graveside on the afternoon of 30 July 1890, a hot day, Dr Gachet spoke.

'He was an honest man and a great artist. He had only two aims, mankind and art.' Weeping, he offered his prognosis. 'Art he loved above everything, and it will make him live.'

Landscape in the Rain

Painted 1890
50 × 100 cm
National Museum of Wales

CHRONOLOGY

1852
30 March – Vincent Willem, son of Revd. Theodorus van Gogh and Anna Carbentus, born dead.

1853
30 March – Vincent Willem van Gogh born in Groot Zundert, Barbant. Three of his uncles were art dealers.

1857
1 May – Theo van Gogh born.

1861
Attends village school.

1864–1866
Sent to a private boarding school at Zevenbergen.

1866
September – attends Willem II Rijks Hogere Burgerschool in Tilburg.

1869
30 July – becomes an assistant in the Hague branch of Paris art dealers Goupil & Co.

1872
Begins correspondence with Theo (who is still at school).

1873
May – transferred by Goupils to their London branch; from lodges at 87 Hackford Road, Stockwell, South London.

1874
June – holidays with his parents at Helvoist. 'Lately I took up drawing again'.
July – returns to London with his sister Anna; in August is rejected by Eugenie Loyer, his landlady's daughter.
November – transfers to Goupils in Paris.

1875
January – returns to London; then in May is transferred again to Paris.
December – visits Etten for Christmas. Returns to Paris and is dismissed.

1876
14 April – becomes an assistant teacher in a school in Ramsgate, Kent, run by William Stokes.
June – walks to Welwyn, north of London, to see his sister Anna, then to Isleworth where Stokes opens a new school.
July – joins Revd. Thomas Slade-Jones' school 'Holme Court'.
5 November – preaches first sermon at Richmond Methodist Church, Kew Road.
December – visits Etten for Christmas and decides not to return to London.

1877
January – works for a Dordrecht bookseller, a job arranged by his Uncle Vincent.

May – moves to Amsterdam to study Greek and Latin for university entrance. Lodges with his Uncle Jan, Director of the shipyards.

1878
July – stops studying and moves to theological college at Laeken near Brussels. He fails to qualify and returns to Etten.
December – leaves for Borinage in South Belgium to become a temporary preacher in Wasmes. He goes down into the mines, and sides with strikers. His appointment is not renewed.

1879
August – works on his own as a preacher at Cuesmes near Mons. He is destitute and estranged from Theo for nine months.

1880
August – stops missionary work to become an artist, supported by an allowance from Theo who has begun working for Goupils. Copies Millet. Ambition to become 'the illustrator of the people'.
October – enrols at Art Academy in Brussels.

1881
April – in Etten rows with his father over becoming an artist.
August – falls in love with his cousin Kee Vos, but is rejected.
November – lives in The Hague. Tutored for a while by his cousin by marriage, the Hague School painter Anton Mauve, he produces his first paintings, still lives.
December – quarrels with Mauve.

1882
January – meets prostitute Sien Hoornik and takes her in. His Uncle Cornelius commissions drawings of The Hague.
August – Theo provides money for paint and canvas.

1883
September – leaving Sien behind, goes to Drenthe in the East Netherlands, staying in Hoogeveen and Nieuw Amsterdam.
December – returns to his parents in Nuenen.

1884
January – nurses his mother while she is laid up with a broken leg. Involvement with Margot Bergeman ends when she attempts suicide.

1885
Makes studies of weavers and of the De Groot family in 1884–5.
27 March – Theodorus van Gogh dies.
June – Plans to paint a series of fifty heads. Priest forbids the villagers of Nuenen to sit for him.
October – spends three days in Amsterdam, studying Frans Hals.
27 November – moves to Antwerp and enrols at Art Academy. Fills the walls of his room at 194 rue des Images with Japanese prints acquired in the docks. Infected with syphilis. Loses teeth.

1886
Arriving in Paris for the first time in ten years he meets Theo, as planned, in the Salon Carré at the Louvre. They live first in the

rue Laval, then in a third-floor apartment at 54 rue Lepic in Montmartre.

March–June – attends Atelier Cormon, where he meets Emile Bernard and Toulouse-Lautrec. Copies antique statuary in the afternoons. Meets Gauguin.

1887

January – meets Père Tanguy, colour-merchant. Arranges two exhibitions at the Café Tambourin: Japanese prints and works by Anquetin, Bernard, Toulouse-Lautrec and himself.

May–July – painting trips, sometimes with Signac, to the suburb of Asnières.

1888

February – encouraged by Lautrec's accounts of the Midi, and following Gauguin's example, leaves Paris.

21 February – arrives in Arles and takes a room in Café de l'Alcazar, Place Lamartine.

March – writes to Gauguin suggesting an association of painters. Has two landscapes exhibited in the Salon des Indépendants.

May – takes two rooms in the 'Yellow House'. Asks Gauguin to come and work with him. Goes on sketching excursions with Lieutenant Milliet.

11–25 June – makes a trip to Les Saintes-Maries-de-la-Mer. 'Now that I have seen the sea here I am absolutely convinced of the importance of staying in the Midi, and of absolutely piling on, exaggerating the colour – Africa not so far away.'

September – with money from a legacy left to Theo, buys furniture for the Yellow House.

17 September – moves into the Yellow House.

23 October – Gauguin arrives in Arles.

Mid-December – visits Montpellier with Gauguin. Theo tells Vincent about his engagement to Johanna Bonger.

23 December – mutilates his left ear, following a row with Gauguin and takes the lobe to Rachel in 'Maison de Tolerance 1'. Joseph Roulin helps him home. The police send him to the hospital 'Hôtel-Dieu'.

25 December – Theo arrives, summoned by a telegram from Gauguin who leaves with him a day or two later.

1889

7 January – allowed home, though has to return to the hospital daily to have the wound dressed. Roulin is transferred to Marseilles. Paints several versions of his portrait of Madame Roulin, *La Berceuse*.

5 February – suffers another collapse.

19 March – confined to hospital, where he is later visited by Signac and Roulin. Doctor Rey secures him new lodgings.

17 April – Theo and Jo Bonger marry. Talks of suicide, joining the Foreign Legion, or of being placed in an asylum.

8 May – moves to Asylum of Saint Paul de Mausole at Saint-Rémy, escorted by Pastor Salles. Admitted as 'third-class

inmate', to 'prevent a recurrence of previous attacks'.

5 July – Jo writes to tell him she is pregnant.

6 July – goes to Arles to collect and send off to Theo paintings left in the Yellow House. Sees Rachel. While returning to Saint-Rémy becomes delirious.

10 July – another crisis renders him unable to paint until the end of August.

September – starts planning to return North.

December – has a breakdown, again associated with Christmas.

1890

January – 'Les Isolés', an article by Albert Aurier, Symbolist poet, about van Gogh, appears in *Mercure de France*.

31 January – birth of Vincent Willem van Gogh, to Theo and Jo.

February – after a further breakdown, tells his mother he is longing to return to the North.

March – *Red Vines* is sold for 400 francs at the exhibition of 'Les XX' in Brussels.

16 May – leaves Saint-Rémy after more than a fortnight of rapid and brilliant work. In all van Gogh completes 150 paintings and 100 drawings at Saint-Rémy.

17 May – arrives in Paris. Stays with Theo, meeting Jo for the first time. Sees Père Tanguy and others and looks through his accumulated work.

20 May – goes to Auvers-sur-Oise. Takes a room above the Café Ravoux in the Place de la Mairie, with another room to paint in. Meets Dr Gachet.

8 June – Theo and Jo come to see him, bringing the baby to whom he gives a bird's nest.

6 July – visits Theo in Paris. Learns that they plan to return to Holland. Lunches with Lautrec, sees Aurier; returns to Auvers disturbed.

20 May–27 July – completes seventy paintings and thirty drawings.

27 July – shoots himself in the chest. Returns to the Café and goes up to his room.

28 July – Theo is summoned to Auvers.

29 July – at 1.30 am, Vincent van Gogh dies, aged thirty-seven. A letter to Theo is found in his pocket. 'Well, the truth is, we can only make our pictures speak.'

30 July – the funeral is attended by Theo, Dr Gachet, Ravoux (owner of the café), Père Tanguy, Emile Bernard.

1891

25 January – Theo van Gogh dies, in Utrecht, aged thirty-four.

SELECT BIBLIOGRAPHY

DE LA FAILLE, J.-B. *The Works of Vincent van Gogh*, Amsterdam, 1970.

HAMMACHER, A.M. *Van Gogh: A Documentary Biography*, London, 1982.

HULSKER, Jan *The Complete van Gogh: Paintings Drawings Sketches*, Amsterdam, 1978: Oxford and New York, 1980.

TRALBAUT, Marc *Vincent van Gogh*, London and New York, 1969.

VAN GOGH, Vincent *The Complete Letters of Vincent van Gogh*, 3 vols., introduction by V.W. van Gogh, London and New York, 1958.

EXHIBITION CATALOGUES

English Influences on Vincent van Gogh, Ronald Pickvance, London, 1974.

Van Gogh in Arles, Ronald Pickvance, Metropolitan Museum, New York, 1984.

Van Gogh in Saint-Rémy and Anvers, Ronald Pickvance, Metropolitan Museum, New York, 1986.

Van Gogh à Paris, Musée d'Orsay, Paris, 1988.

LIST OF PLATES

All works are by Vincent van Gogh.

4 *Self-Portrait*, Oct/Dec 1887. Oil on canvas, 47 × 35 cm. Musée d'Orsay, Paris. © Photo: R.M.N.

7 *The Carpenter's Yard and Laundry*, 1882. Black chalk heightened with white, 28.5 × 47 cm. Rijksmuseum Kröller-Müller, Otterlo.

8 *The Yellow House in Arles*, September 1888. Chalk, pen, brown ink, watercolour, 25.5 × 31.5 cm. Vincent van Gogh Foundation, Vincent van Gogh Museum, Amsterdam.

10 *Red Vineyards at Arles*, 1888. Oil on canvas, 75 × 93 cm. Pushkin Museum, Moscow. Photo: SCALA.

11 *The Dance Hall at Arles*, December 1888. Oil on canvas, 65 × 81 cm. Musée d'Orsay, Paris. © Photo: R.M.N.

12 *Women Carrying Coal*, autumn 1882. Watercolour, 32 × 50 cm. Rijksmuseum Kröller-Müller, Otterlo.

13 *Portrait of the Artist's Mother*, October 1888. Oil on canvas, Norton Simon Art Foundation.

14 *Mademoiselle Gachet in her Garden*, June 1890. Oil on canvas, 46 × 55 cm. Musée d'Orsay, Paris. © Photo: R.M.N.

15 *The Chair*, 1890. Pencil, 33 × 24.5 cm. Vincent van Gogh Foundation, Vincent van Gogh Museum, Amsterdam.

16 *Garden in Provence*, July 1888. Pen drawing, 49 × 61 cm. Collection Oskar Reinhart, Am Römerholz, Winterthur.

17 *Meadow with Butterflies*, May 1890. Oil on canvas, 64.5 × 91 cm. National Gallery, London.

19 *Pollard Willows and Setting Sun*, October 1888. Oil on canvas, 31.5 × 34.5 cm. Rijksmuseum Kröller-Müller, Otterlo.

21 *St Paul's Hospital, Saint-Rémy*, 1889. Oil on canvas, 63 × 48 cm. Musée d'Orsay, Paris. © Photo: R.M.N.

22 *Street in Auvers-sur-Oise*, 1890. Oil on canvas, 73 × 92 cm. Ateneum, Antell Collection. Photo: The Finnish National Gallery.

23 *Thatched Cottages in Auvers*, July 1890. Oil on canvas, 65 × 81 cm. Kunsthaus, Zurich.

25 *Sunflowers*, 1887. Oil on canvas, 43.2 × 61 cm. Metropolitan Museum of Art, Rogers Fund, 1949.

27 *Drawbridge with Carriage*, 1888. Oil on canvas, 54.5 × 65 cm. Rijksmuseum Kröller-Müller, Otterlo.

29 *Orchard with Blossoming Plum Trees*, 1888. Drawing in red ink, 39.5 × 54 cm. Vincent van Gogh Foundation, Vincent van Gogh Museum, Amsterdam.

31 *The Old Peasant, Patience Escalier*, 1888. Oil on canvas, 64 × 54 cm. Private Collection. Photo: Bridgeman Art Library.

33 *Public Garden with Round Clipped Shrub and Weeping Tree (The Garden of the Poets)*, 1888. Oil on canvas, 73 × 92 cm. Mr and Mrs Lewis Larned Coburn Memorial Collection, 1933. Photo: © 1992. All rights reserved, The Art Institute of Chicago.

35 Sketch for *Starry Night*, September 1888. Vincent van Gogh Foundation, Vincent van Gogh Museum, Asmterdam.

37 *Portrait of Armand Roulin*, 1888. Oil on canvas, 66 × 55 cm. Folkwang Museum, Essen.

39 *Irises*, 1889. Oil on canvas, 71 × 93 cm. Collection of the J. Paul Getty Museum, Malibu, California.

41 *Enclosed Field with Reaper at Sunrise*, 1889. Oil on canvas, 59.5 × 73 cm. Folkwang Museum, Essen.

42 Photograph of Vincent van Gogh. Vincent van Gogh Foundation, Vincent van Gogh Museum, Amsterdam.

45 *Peasant Burning Weeds*, 1833. Oil on panel, 30.5 × 39.5 cm. Rijksmuseum Kröller-Müller, Otterlo.

47 *The Potato Eaters*, 1885. Oil on canvas, 82 × 114 cm. Vincent van Gogh Foundation, Vincent van Gogh Museum, Amsterdam.

49 *Peasant Cemetery*, 1885. Oil on canvas, 63 × 79 cm. Vincent van Gogh Foundation, Vincent van Gogh Museum, Amsterdam.

51 *Still Life with Open Bible, Candlestick and Novel*, 1885. Oil on canvas, 63 × 78 cm. Vincent van Gogh Foundation, Vincent van Gogh Museum, Amsterdam.

53 *Le Moulin de Blute-Fin, Montmartre*, 1886. Oil on canvas, 45.4 × 37.5 cm. Glasgow Art Gallery and Museum.

55 *A Basket of Bulbs*, 1887. Oil on panel, 31.5 × 48 cm. Vincent van Gogh Foundation, Vincent van Gogh Museum, Amsterdam.

57 *A Pair of Shoes*, 1887. Oil on canvas, 34 × 41.5 cm. Baltimore Museum of Art.

59 *Skull*, 1887/8. Oil on canvas, 41.5 × 31.5 cm. Vincent van Gogh Foundation, Vincent van Gogh Museum, Amsterdam.

61 *Self-Portrait with Straw Hat*, 1887. Oil on cardboard, 41 × 33 cm. Vincent van Gogh Foundation, Vincent van Gogh Museum, Amsterdam.

63 *Portrait of Père Tanguy*, 1887/8. Oil on canvas, 92 × 75 cm. Musée Rodin, Paris.

65 *Blossoming Almond in a Glass*, 1888. Oil on canvas, 24 × 19 cm. Vincent van Gogh Foundation, Vincent van Gogh Museum, Amsterdam.

67 *Field with Flowers*, 1888. Oil on canvas, 54 × 65 cm. Vincent van Gogh Foundation, Vincent van Gogh Museum, Amsterdam.

69 *Harvest Landscape*, 1888. Oil on canvas, 72.5 × 92 cm. Vincent van Gogh Foundation, Vincent van Gogh Museum, Amsterdam.

71 *Haystacks Near a Farm*, 1888. Oil on canvas, 73 × 92.5 cm. Rijksmuseum Kröller-Müller, Otterlo.

73 *Sower with Setting Sun*, 1888. Oil on canvas, 64 × 80.5 cm. Rijksmuseum Kröller-Müller, Otterlo.

75 *Mousmé Sitting in a Cane Chair, Half-Figure*, 1888. Oil on canvas, 74 × 60 cm. National Gallery of Art, Washington, Chester Dale Collection.

77 *Joseph Roulin, Sitting in a Cane Chair, Three-Quarter Length*, 1888. Oil on canvas, 81 × 65 cm. Museum of Fine Art, Boston, gift of Robert Treat Pain II.

79 *The Night Café*, 1888. Oil on canvas, 70 × 89 cm. Yale University Art Gallery, bequest of Simon Carlton Clark, B.A., 1903.

81 *Café Terrace at Night*, 1888. Oil on canvas, 81 × 65.5 cm. Rijksmuseum Kröller-Müller, Otterlo.

83 *Fourteen Sunflowers in a Vase*, 1888. Oil on canvas, 93 × 73 cm. National Gallery, London.

85 *Lieutenant Milliet*, 1888. Oil on canvas, 60 × 49 cm. Rijksmuseum Kröller-Müller, Otterlo.

87 *Les Alyscamps*, 1888. Oil on canvas, 73 × 92 cm. Rijksmuseum Kröller-Müller, Otterlo.

89 *Vincent's Chair*, 1888. Oil on canvas, 93 × 73.5 cm. National Gallery, London.

91 *Gauguin's Chair*, 1888. Oil on canvas, 90.5 × 72 cm.

Vincent van Gogh Foundation, Vincent van Gogh Museum, Amsterdam.

93 *Augustine Roulin (La Berceuse)*, 1888–9. Oil on canvas, 92 × 73 cm. Rijksmuseum Kröller-Müller, Otterlo.

95 *Still Life with Onions and Book*, 1889. Oil on canvas, 50 × 64 cm. Rijksmuseum Kröller-Müller, Otterlo.

97 *Self-Portrait with Bandaged Ear*, 1889. Oil on canvas, 60 × 49 cm. Courtauld Institute Galleries, (Courtauld Collection), London. Photo: Bridgeman Art Library.

99 *The Crau with Peach in Bloom*, 1889. Oil on canvas, 65.5 × 81.5 cm. Courtauld Institute Galleries, (Courtauld Collection), London. Photo: Bridgeman Art Library.

101 *Dormitory in Hospital*, 1889. Oil on canvas, 74 × 92 cm. Private Collection.

103 *Mountain Landscape Seen across the Walls with Rising Sun and Green Field*, 1889. Oil on canvas, 72 × 92 cm. Rijksmuseum Kröller-Müller, Otterlo.

105 *Wheat Field with Cypresses*, 1889. Oil on canvas, 72 × 91 cm. National Gallery, London.

107 *Starry Night*, 1889. Oil on canvas, 73 × 92 cm. Museum of Modern Art, New York, acquired through the Lillie P. Bliss Bequest.

109 *Self-Portrait*, 1889. Oil on canvas, 65 × 54 cm. Musée d'Orsay, Paris. © Photo: R.M.N.

111 *Pietà (after Delacroix)*, 1889. Oil on canvas, 73 × 60.5 cm. Vincent van Gogh Foundation, Vincent van Gogh Museum, Amsterdam.

113 *The Artist's Bedroom in Arles*, 1889. Oil on canvas, 56.5 × 74 cm. Musée d'Orsay, Paris. © Photo: R.M.N.

115 *The Ravine*, 1889. Oil on canvas, 73 × 92 cm. Rijksmuseum Kröller-Müller, Otterlo.

117 *Noon: Rest (after Millet)*, 1890. Oil on canvas, 73 × 92 cm. Musée d'Orsay, Paris. © Photo: R.M.N.

119 *Prisoners' Round (after Doré)*, 1890. Oil on canvas, 80 × 64 cm. Pushkin Museum, Moscow. Photo: SCALA.

121 *Branches of an Almond Tree in Blossom*, 1890. Oil on canvas, 73 × 92 cm. ·Vincent van Gogh Foundation, Vincent van Gogh Museum, Amsterdam.

123 *Vase with Violet Irises*, 1890. Oil on canvas, 92 × 73.5 cm. Metropolitan Museum, New York.

125 *Road with Men Walking*, 1890. Oil on canvas, 92 × 73 cm. Rijksmuseum Kröller-Müller, Otterlo.

127 *The Church in Auvers*, 1890. Oil on canvas, 94 × 74 cm. Musée d'Orsay, Paris. © Photo: R.M.N.

129 *Doctor Gachet*, 1890. Oil on canvas, 68 × 57 cm. Musée d'Orsay, Paris. © Photo: R.M.N.

131 *Marguerite Gachet at the Piano*, 1890. Oil on canvas, 102 × 50 cm. Kunstmuseum, Basel. Photo: Colorphoto Hinz, Allschwil.

133 *Landscape with Carriage and Train in the Distance*, 1890. Oil on canvas, 72 × 90 cm. Pushkin Museum, Moscow. Photo: SCALA.

135 *Ears of Wheat*, 1790. Oil on canvas, 64.5 × 47 cm. Vincent van Gogh Foundation, Vincent van Gogh Museum, Amsterdam.

137 *Wheat Field under Threatening Skies*, 1890. Oil on canvas, 50.5 × 100.5 cm. Vincent van Gogh Foundation, Vincent van Gogh Museum, Amsterdam.

139 *Landscape in the Rain*, 1890. Oil on canvas, 50 × 100 cm. Vincent van Gogh Foundation, of Wales.